Telling the American Story:

*A Structural and Cultural Analysis
of Conversational Storytelling*

language and being

edited by
George Lakoff
and
John Robert Ross

A. L. BECKER AND ARAM A. YENGOYAN ● *The Imagination of Reality: Essays in Southeast Asian Coherence Systems,* 1979

WILLIAM E. COOPER ● *Speech Perception and Production: Studies in Selective Adaptation,* 1979

ANN BORKIN ● *Problems in Form and Function,* 1984

LIVIA POLANYI ● *Telling the American Story: A Structural and Cultural Analysis of Conversational Storytelling,* 1985

JOHN ROBERT ROSS ● *Infinite Syntax!*

Telling
The
American Story:

A Structural and Cultural Analysis
of Conversational Storytelling

Livia Polanyi

University of Amsterdam
The Netherlands

ABLEX PUBLISHERS CORPORATION
NORWOOD, NEW JERSEY 07648

Library of Congress Cataloging in Publication Data

Polanyi, Livia.
  Telling the American story.

  (Language and being)
  Based on the author's thesis (Ph.D.)—University of Michigan.
  Bibilography: p.
  Includes index.
  1. Discourse analysis, Narrative.   2. Content analysis
(Communication)   3. United States—Popular culture.
  I. Title.   II. Series.
  P302.P62   1985   401'.41   84-24196
  ISBN 0-89391-041-4

Printed in the United States of America

Ablex Publishing Corporation
355 Chestnut Street
Norwood, New Jersey 07648

CONTENTS

For My Parents

ACKNOWLEDGMENTS

In the five years which have elapsed since finishing the doctoral dissertation upon which this book is based, I have had many doubts about the success of this attempt to unite a linguistic and interactional analysis of conversational stories with a cultural analysis of the most fundamental "truths" upon which we base our stories and, indeed, our decisions and perceptions of the world. I would not undertake this book now. It seems too naive an undertaking and too ambitious a task. Yet I will publish it now in hopes that it may inform the growing field of discourse–level linguistics in some way—if only to indicate both the necessity and difficulty of taking seriously the challenge presented to the linguist, the sociologist, the anthropologist by even the most humble human "artistic" productions in which we seem to be telling each other only "what happened" at a highway restaurant, in the New York subway, or while walking home late at night.

I will always be in debt to the tellers of these stories and to Professors William Labov and Deborah Tannen who allowed me to use stories which they had collected. Professor's Labov's influence on this book extends far beyond supplying "The Baddest Girl in the Neighborhood", however. The linguistic methodology used in this book is very largely a refinement of the ideas on narrative analysis which Labov presented in two seminal papers, "Narrative Analysis," written with Joshua Waletzky (1967), and "The Transformation of Experience in Narrative Syntax" (1972). The discussion of conversational storytelling is most strongly influenced by the work of Harvey Sacks (1970–1) and Gail Jefferson (1978), while the cultural exploration in the latter part of the book could not have had either its form or content without the disturbing and highly suggestive work of both Erving Goffman and Gregory Bateson.

On a more personal note, it is almost impossible to thank the people who have helped and encouraged me both during the writing of the dissertation and during the past years. I should like to mention a few of them specifically. My dissertation advisor, Pete Becker, of the Linguistics Department of the University of Michigan, first allowed and then so gently demanded that I go out on any number of intellectual limbs to see if they would bear the weight of my exploration. My colleagues and students at the University of Amsterdam have taught me that one need not go so far from home to be in a very different world. My friends and family have proven to me that it is possible to go very far away and still be at home. Finally and especially, Ellen, Remko and Ruth fought tirelessly with the structure of this story and were endlessly supportive to the teller.

Eindhoven, The Netherlands
December, 1982

1.

STORIES AS CULTURAL TEXTS (NOT ALL STORIES ARE AMERICAN STORIES)

1.0 INTRODUCTION: AMERICAN STORIES

This book has two themes: the linguistic and social constraints on telling stories in American conversational interactions, and the cultural presuppositions which, taken together, constitute what can be thought of as the "American world view." The title of the book, *The American Story,* is a pun. In the discussion which follows, the conversational stories provide material from which cultural primitives of the more general American Cultural Story are derived.

My basic premise is that people do not choose to talk to each other at length "about" matters which are not of some interest to them. Doing so would be inappropriate behavior, because in taking time to deal with issues that one would not reasonably imagine could be of interest to another, the speaker would be demonstrating improper socialization. A "proper" storyteller, one whose stories are received as normal and reasonable contributions to a conversation already underway, will therefore tell stories whose "points" do not ignore generally accepted truths about the nature of things, but which, rather, relate to them in some fashion. Starting from this viewpoint, I argue that stories can provide useful insight into what matters to those for whom the story is a "normal" "acceptable," "understandable," commonplace production.[1]

This question of determining what a text is "about" is far from simple. Most analyses of stories are content analyses of one sort or another. In such an analysis, a

---

[1]I do not believe that the method of cultural analysis which I am proposing here is, by any means, the only way to reach cultural primitives. As contemporary anthropology makes clear, there are many. However, I do believe that an associative expansion of the obvious is one important method. Similarly, while many source texts can provide insight into a culture, I believe that conversational stories and tales are one widely available access route to folk truths and values.

1

story is approached by saying "Well, this, and this and that are all mentioned in the story and therefore the story must be "about" this and this and that." Stories are composed of many "thisses and thats", however. They are made up of numerous events and states of affairs involving numerous characters and situations. Content analyses of all sorts have failed to justify precisely why some "thisses and thats" are what the story is "about" and others are not.

A determination of what is important, what is seized upon as important, is made not by naming elements themselves, but by understanding the importance of those elements to the point which the teller is making in telling the story. Tellers are very aware of the need to separate out more salient information from less salient information as they are recounting their stories. They display great sensitivity in assigning different weights to the different propositions in the storyworld through the rhetorical markings assigned to each one. Therefore, in this study, a methodology is presented which, beginning with transcripts of conversational stories, produces a paraphrase of the story as told by means of careful attention to the details of encoding the various propositions about what went on when and why in the storyworld. This paraphrase consists only of those elements which the teller most heavily foregrounded in the telling. Such a paraphrase, which can be used in investigations of all sorts, from narrative analysis to psycholinguistic studies of memory, is used in the present case as an object for cultural analysis.

In the fourth chapter of this book, "The World Evoked by American Stories," the propositions composing the paraphrase of the conversational stories discussed in the earlier chapters are expanded into a discussion of basic American values and beliefs. This expansion is done by asking what is most interesting, storyworthy, or compelling about the elements in the propositions themselves.[2] The presuppositions structuring the expansion text are themselves then distilled and organized into an abstract, formal American Cultural Grammar. This, in its turn, is used generatively in the last chapter to produce a generic American Story consisting of "Basic Truths" about the nature of the world and the proper conduct of human relationships. This study can therefore be considered a generative cultural exegesis in which texts are produced from other texts, expanded, distilled into their elements, which are themselves expanded into a text to be subjected to the same processes of abstraction into elementary propositions. This is always the case in the social sciences, but seldom so explicitly.

In expanding the propositions in the stories themselves (which were, with one exception, told in undirected conversations among American born, English speaking, white, middle class friends) I have used myself, a reasonably acculturated native-born

---

[2]An analyst wishing to examine the stories of a culture not his own using the linguistic methodology presented here would need to make use of a cultural initiate to expand the story propositions into a thick text, precisely as a linguist investigating the grammar of a language other than his own must make use of a native speaker informant to make the important grammaticality decisions. Otherwise, the would-be analyst is likely to build up a composite picture of what *he* would have found interesting about the story materials had he told stories in which they figured prominently and would surely miss almost entirely the impact of the various goings-on in the storyworld on the teller and others who share his world view.

American, as an informant. In doing so, I was operating within the tradition of transformational grammarians who have long used their own "native speaker intuitions" as a source of insight into the syntactic acceptability of sentences in their own languages. My ordinary judgments are correct insofar as the resulting text seems a string of clichés to my compatriots. Insofar as another cultural American finds himself surprised by an observation, I have failed to capture the "unintentionally obvious." These self-evident "everyone knows this" truths differ tremendously from culture to culture. Because we always base our linguistic texts upon these implicitly assumed notions, genuine, satisfactory cross-cultural communication is most unlikely if, indeed, it is possible at all. This book, therefore, will, like all other texts, be one sort of "story" for those who share my cultural presuppositions (if not my scientific standpoint) and it must necessarily be quite another text for those who do not. This does not mean that we cannot profit enormously from interactions with those different from ourselves—lest this be taken as a plea for xenophobia—but we must accept that the interaction we are having with them is necessarily different from the interaction they are having with us—even with the best will in the world.

1.1 AMERICAN TEXTS AND AMERICAN VALUES

This book, written by an American, is, itself, an American text which consistently reveals the cultural origin of its producer. The choice of subject, the nature of the argumentation, the tone and style of its presentation, even this self-reflexive meta-comment, all declare it to be an American text—perhaps more insistently to one who is not an American than to someone who is. Rather than treat this book as autonomous and anonymous, I will sometimes intrude upon the discourse. While this is unusual in scientific discussions, I cannot justify separating myself from the analysis which necessarily resulted in large part from my own Americanness. A stance of scientific impersonality, while surely more comfortable in many ways than the unconventional stance adopted here, weakens a cultural exploration, especially of one's own culture, because it deprives those who wish to understand the analytic process of much valuable data which could be used in constructing models of the target culture.

Having said this, then, I would now like to share some of the experiences which have brought home to me, in the years since completing the research on which this book is based, how American I really am, how a part of one's formative culture every human being ultimately is, and how decisive a role cultural conditioning plays in the construction and interpretation of linguistic and behavioral texts.

The data on which this book is based came from hours of tape-recorded conversations of my friends talking casually at dinner, in the evening after a party, to one another, and to me. I found it relatively easy to ask them if I might make use of our social interactions for my work. That my work was almost always on my mind seemed natural for me and for them, and they had no difficulty granting me permission to tape them freely. Yes, of course, they wanted to see exactly which texts I would pick to analyze and were often curious to read what I wrote about them, but they did not feel I was acting inappropriately in "working" as we were visiting with one another. In many other cultures, even in Western European countries which seem to resemble North America in many ways, such a redefinition of a social situation into a "work" situation would not be possible even among serious-minded academics with similar interests and background. In Holland, for example, where I have been living and working for the past few years, to "use" one's friends for research and analysis would be viewed by most academics as a violation of the social contract. A thoughtless, selfish act in which one person put one's own personal wants and needs above the well-being of others.

Of course, like any expatriate, I can tell endless stories of misunderstandings and difficulties I have had trying to adjust to living and working Someplace Else, even an Else as comfortable, as affluent, as modern, and as genuinely decent as The Netherlands. But I will restrain myself and tell only one story which describes the experience through which I became aware of the differences between Dutch and American attitudes towards the concept of "work"—not towards the performance of work-related activities—but towards the role which "work" should properly play in one's life and in one's discourse.

After I had been in Holland for a while, I noticed that something odd happened in a conversation when I was asked how I had come to find myself there more or less permanently. At first, I had treated this question as more or less unproblematic. I would explain that I was there because of my job. Basically, I would say, I had acquired my job through an ad in an American professional journal asking for someone with my qualifications. Needing a job, and intrigued by the promise of an interview in Amsterdam, I answered the ad, was interviewed in Holland, and was hired on the spot. So, I ended up moving to Holland and had been there since. I would then be quite confused when my questioner would persist in asking me again why I had come to Holland. Patiently, I would explain that the job was suited to my interests and that I had a chance to teach and do research in my particular specializa-tions. "Oh," I would hear, and the conversation would immediately shift to some very neutral or business-related topic and I would feel a definite sense of disappointment and distance emanating from my interlocutors.

After having had this experience a number of times over a couple of years, I finally asked some native informants what was going on. Why had they found my answer so bewildering, so off-putting? Since they were students in my seminar on Dutch and American cultural values, where this sort of question was more or less appropriate, they explained, after looking at each other nervously for a while, that they really had wanted to know why I had come. I told them that I had just explained why I had come. They then explained that they had felt a bit let down and betrayed by my answer; they had considered their daring to ask the question at all a sign of their willingness to accept the offer of relative intimacy and informality which my Ameri-can classroom manner promised. When I had given an answer telling them only about my work, they felt as if I had rejected them, refusing to give an honest answer. "After all," they said. "There must be a *real* reason why you left America and chose to come here." When I asked what sort of "real" reason they had in mind, they suggested that perhaps I liked the political situation or cultural atmosphere in Europe better than that in the United States, or perhaps I thought that Holland was more beautiful than America.

We discussed their expectations and my answer for quite a while, and gradually it became clear that what I had given as (conventional) valid reasons for an important life decision struck them as evasive and irrelevant, "not real." And on my part, and from what I find an unexceptional American perspective, it would never have occurred to me that answers which would ring true in Holland would involve my personal life only and neither professional nor intellectual considerations. After a bit more exploration, it became clear that another reason which would have been quite acceptable might have involved money; had the job in Holland paid better than one in the United States I could have used the financial reason without further explanation.

The reasons I had given, however, all related to my "work", were almost incomprehensible. How could anyone leave friends, family and home behind to come to Holland only for "work"? And if it were really the case that I had done so, how could I possibly admit so casually, so callously, to being "ambitious" (which is very very badly thought of in Holland). And not only ambitious, but a *vakidioot* to boot. (*vakidioot* is the sort of untranslatable word which always appears in anecdotes of this kind. It can be glossed as "a one sided academic grind who is interested only in his field.") Who would willingly present herself as a *vakidioot*—someone poorly socialized, boring, and selfish, who thinks and talks about only what she is interested in and does not take into account the fact that other people may be bored by her work? In Holland, the presupposition is that people are only interested in what *they* know and are therefore obviously bored by someone else's field. It is rude to discuss a subject with which you are extremely familiar with people who know little about it. It is considered polite to talk about only common rather than "specialized" subjects in a social situation, even with colleagues, while to talk about a work-related interest would seem very one-sided and rude.

So, my conventional, impersonal, unimpeachable American explanation of why I went to Holland was, for my Dutch hosts, completely unconventional, potentially overly-revealing and socially incomprehensible. While I was giving an explanation which presented a self which was rational, sensible, businesslike, work-oriented, committed and serious, they were hearing about a self which was cold, calculating, uncaring, work-obsessed, ambitious, and slightly inhuman. They could only believe that I was rejecting their attempts at intimacy by giving them a story which could not possibly be believed, thereby signalling them that they were coming too close in asking me a personal question. The alternative, even more disturbing, was that I was showing much more of my "true self" than was appropriate, that they had come too close to someone no reasonable Dutch person would want to be associated with.

This is one of (unfortunately) the endless examples of bungled cross-cultural communications I might have chosen. In telling this story I am *not* claiming that Dutch and American people necessarily do things for different reasons (which they may well do, but that is properly the subject of a separate investigation). I am claiming, however, that the *reasons* which are acceptable to give in explaining or justifying one's actions are often different among the two peoples. Dutch discourse is sufficiently different from American discourse so that a "normal" story in one culture is often not a "normal" story in the other. Just as jokes seldom travel well, the everyday conversational story, commonplace justification, argument, or explanation is often (unpredictably) less successful abroad than at home. Attempting to find out how the same text might be interpreted by members of two different cultures can lead an analyst quite far afield from the original text. Just now, we have needed to trace the connotations of words and chase up and down the paths of cultural reasoning to explain what was going on in the cross-cultural "communication breakdown" described above. In other words, in order to make sense out of everyday conversational texts, one ends up engaged in the entire anthropological enterprise of figuring out what a set of texts in a given culture "means" and how that meaning is communicated through the structure of the texts.

1.2 A NOTE ABOUT "AMERICANS"

Conversational stories are highly structured linguistic productions. The information conventionally included in storytellings is organized in highly predictable ways, as shall be discussed at length in subsequent chapters. However, before going on to technical discussions of narrative structure, it is important to consider the nature of the "Americans" included within the scope of the claims about story structure, conversational behavior, and world view presented in this book.

I am an educated, middle class, white, adult woman. Most of the tellers of the stories in this book are women of similar background. A number, too, are "East Coast Jews" who share with me a number of stylistic conversational characteristics of the type discussed by Tannen (1984). All tellers have English as a first language and none have strong ties outside of "mainstream" Middle-American society, except for the adolescent narrator of "The Baddest Girl in the Neighborhood," who is a member of the Philadelphia inner city Black community.[3]

In gathering stories for this book, I did not attempt to find a cross-section of speakers. All of the tellers, as it turns out, are Northerners, all are urban or suburban dwellers, and all but one are adults who are reasonably well-off financially—although none are extremely well-to-do. Although the influence of race, class, sex, age, or other social factors of importance in storytelling as well as all other forms of communication and interaction are not dealt with in this book, this does not mean that I do not

[3]This story was collected by W. Labov and is used here with his permission.

appreciate their importance in shaping linguistic productions or life experience. American society is far from homogenous, of course, and there are very different norms of behavior and strong differences of opinion about style of life and the relative importance of some values over others among different segments of American society. However, in this study I examine only those aspects of American life and thought basic to being a socialized, reasonably acculturated person in America.

These values underlie political slogans and lie below the surface in advertising campaigns. They persuade Americans of all races, classes, and educational levels to support candidates, to desire, to buy. Those values are in *Ebony* and *Jet* no less than in *Time, Newsweek,* or *The Ladies' Home Journal.* They determine the very issues around which the Black Civil Rights Movement has rallied and informs the rhetoric of the other "mainstream" minority groups in their American demands for "fairness", "justice", "opportunity", "equality" and "freedom." Most assimilated, English speaking, Asian Americans, Gay Americans, Handicapped Americans, Jewish Americans and Female Americans as well as Black Americans and Nonminority Americans accept without question that these "rights" constitute "equality" and "freedom" which are themselves the prerequisites for the "satisfying", "decent" and, above all, "happy" life which each "individual" deserves without question.[4]

From an "insider's" point of view, the social world is composed of distinct subgroups distinguished from one another by clearly relevant criteria such as position, property, customs or beliefs. The outsider, however, does not distinguish one group of insiders from another. The similarities among the Others outweigh and obscure the possible differences, reducing them in the end to insignificance (Lotman, 1978). Let me give one brief example out of my own experience to illustrate Lotman's point.

My students in Amsterdam insist that it is impossible to make any generalizations about "Dutch" culture at all. (They *all* insist as well that making any sort of generalization is wrong.) After all, they say, the various regions of The Netherlands are so different from one another. To be correct, we should talk about rural Dutch culture versus urban Dutch culture (and Amsterdam versus Rotterdam versus the rest of the country). In addition, we must distinguish between "middle class Dutch culture" and "working class Dutch culture" and, of course, "Northern Calvinist Dutch culture" and "Southern (easygoing) Dutch culture." As an outsider in the country, however, I see only the very slightest differences among these groups. For me, the Dutch are one very homogeneous cultural entity. However, I find Americans from the East Coast very different from Americans from the West Coast and Americans from the Mid-

---

[4]Native Americans, unassimilated foreign born, or non-English speaking ethnic minorities as well as some historically isolated rural or religious groups might not accept this complex of assumptions as automatically. They may have alternative world views which allow them to make a very different sort of sense out of their experience than their "American" neighbors. These residents and citizens of the United States are outside of the American "mainstream." They are different, foreign, exotic.

These "exotic" minorities may well see no significant differences among those outside their own group. The "Others" may all be "Americans," "Whitemen," "City Folks," or "Nonbelievers." Those of us within mainstream American society, on the other hand, see many very distinct groups separated from one another and from "our" group by a myriad salient characteristics.

west very different from Americans from either Coast. Black Americans seem very different from White Americans and university–educated Americans very different from Americans with little formal schooling. I find great differences as well between male Americans and female Americans. For my Dutch friends, colleagues and students we are all very much alike. When I ask my students what they find so similar among us all, they tend to get a bit embarrassed and finally reply, in what seems to me a very blunt Dutch way, *"You know*! You're all so incredibly *American."*

2.

THE STRUCTURE OF STORIES

2.0 INTRODUCTION

Competent users of language recognize when a story is being told. In an American conversation, story recipients are alerted by conventional story introducers which a would-be storyteller uses to signal the intention to tell a story. The talk then moves out of the here and now of the conversation into a storyworld: another time, often another location, populated by other participants. The teller makes use of deictic markers in a way which indicates a change of frame of reference and no one is surprised if the narrator speaks from a perspective not his own. All these world-building and world-populating activities are familiar from innumerable other story-tellings. As the telling unfolds, there is a clear expectation that "what happened" in that other time and place will become clear.

In this chapter, the nature of stories in general is explored and the linguistic realization of stories in English is specified in some detail. The discussion provides a methodology for abstracting from the surface structure of a text those propositions about the storyworld which, if taken together, are the essence of the story as told. The significance of the presuppositions upon which these propositions are built to Americans in general will be explored in the concluding sections of this book. This chapter, then, functions as a bridge between the discussion of culture and stories as cultural artifacts of the first chapter and the rest of the book in which cultural constraints on American stories are examined.

2.1 "NARRATIVES" AND "EVENTS"

Stories, along with plans, simultaneous "blow-by-blow" descriptions, generic narratives about "the way it used to be" or "what usually happens" and reports of past activities are all *narratives*—kinds of discourse organized around the passage of time in some "world." In narrative discourse of all sorts, a time line is established, demarcated by discrete moments at which instantaneous occurrences (*events*) take place in the world created through the telling. Although all of the narratives we shall be concerned with will be linguistic texts, narratives are not necessarily linguistically encoded. Narrative films and plays, as well as narrative paintings, music and dance, and narrative poems and jokes are built around a series of events marking the progress of time in the world conjured up by the piece.

In any narrative, some of the events form the *main time line*—a series of successive instants in the narrated world which correspond to the moving reference point in the narrative construction of that world. In a *story,* this reference point is always in the past relative to the time of narrating (even if the time of narrating is assumed to be future to the time of encoding [as in science fiction, for example]). In *plans* the reference point is always future to the planning time, while in *simultaneous narration* the movement of the reference point is synchronized with the actual passage of time in the speech situation. Other events may be off the main time line on a separate time line whose temporal location is established relative to the main line of the ongoing narrative. A *flashback* or *flashahead*, for example, is understood to be "before" or "after" the moment time has reached in the embedding discourse. The time of the "flash" is indicated in some way. (The most common means in a linguistic narrative include tense changes, discourse particles, adverbial clauses, or explicit meta-comments.) An event in a flashed segment is interpreted as establishing a new reference point in the flashed world while the progress of time in the "main" world to which the flash world is related remains unaffected.

Event is used here to mean an occurrence in some world which is described as having an instantaneous rather than a durative or iterative character. In the world's languages, there are means available to indicate events. In the Indo-European languages, including English, this semantic information is carried by the aspectual component of the tense-carrying verb in a clause. Those events syntactically encoded in main clauses form the main time line. *Event clauses* are semantically punctual, noniterative, and completive. In non-Indo-European languages, according to Jones and Jones (1979), and Hopper and Thompson (1980), the distinction between main line event clauses and other clauses may be made with narrative particles or by special morphological marking somewhere on the clause.

Narrative texts are seldom composed only of event clauses, however, but contain stative clauses as well which differ from event clauses in temporal interpretation. Such *state clauses* encode states of affairs which persist over some interval of time in the discourse world rather than occurring at one unique discrete instant.

2.2 NARRATIVE GENRES

Stories and *reports* are specific, affirmative, past time narratives which tell about a series of events (i.e. more than one) which *did* take place at specific unique moments in a unique past time world. The narrative line in these discourse genres in English is built with simple past tense event clauses or with a combination of these clearly past time clauses and morphologically present tense clauses which are given a past time semantic interpretation (the so-called "historical present tense"). The events are specific and affirmative. Event clauses may use transitive or intransitive verbs and tend to have specific agents and objects.

However any given event, agent, or object in a generic narrative, is not unique, but stands for a class of such events, agents, or objects, since the world of the narration is not a unique world, but is rather a class of worlds in which the activities and circumstances described generally obtain. Generic past time narratives are structured around indefinite past time events encoded in event clauses with generic modals such as would or used to. (Joos, 1968) The meaning of an event in a generic past time narrative could be glossed as "It would *always* be the case that at this exact moment in the proceedings, Event X took place."

Similarly, the meaning of an event clause in a generic present time narrative can be glossed "Always, at this exact moment in the proceedings, Event X takes place." This is quite distinct from the semantic interpretation accorded a main line event clause in a simultaneous narration: "At this exact moment in both the narrative world and the world of the narration, Event X is taking place." Although the two "present tense" clauses may be morphologically identical, they are accorded very different interpretations due to clues elsewhere in the discourse.

Plans and other descriptions of wished for but yet unrealized sequences of events and negative narratives which describe a sequence of occurrences which did not or ought not to occur are encoded in event clauses with modal markers indicating the type of assertion being made. Remote past events in otherwise past time narrative genres are often in the pluperfect, although if there are a series of such events, each one need not be so marked. Similarly, in a present time narration, a simple past tense event will establish a time line previous to the moment of time in the embedding discourse. In all cases, however, the clauses capable of initiating or continuing a discrete time line are punctual, noniterative, and completive.

While nonnarrative discourses never include more than one distinct event proposition, there is no limit on the number of state propositions which may legitimately be part of a narrative. States in narratives may come into being at a particular moment or last until a specific time while events in the discourse may act as beginning or end points for the interval of time for which the state obtains. Other states begin or end gradually during a period bracketed by events, while still others end slowly and at an indefinite, unspecified time. States may obtain for a whole narrative or only for the shortest possible interval of time. Some states obtain in the world of narrating as in the world created through the narration; some obtain at all times in all worlds, while others may be less universal in scope.

Conventions of narration, in English, at least, call for universally true propositions to occur early in a telling, followed by more restricted state propositions, followed by a section of event clauses and states restricted to intervals of time in the narrative world. Time in narratives funnels in towards the "NOW" of the narrative genre (towards past time events, in past time narratives; towards the moment of speaking in simultaneous narrations; towards the specific future instants when events are to occur in plans, etc.) As Grimes has shown in his analysis of "The Gettysburg Address," (1982) even nonnarrative discourses may be organized as a temporal progression from the universally true, through those states and events which preceded the moment of narrative center (the RIGHT NOW of the moment the speech was delivered), through to a (possibly indefinite) future time. Unless marked as being "out of place" by some sort of comment or displacement phenomenon (such as the *true start* discussed in Polanyi, 1978b) deviations from this order are used to signal a new *episode* in the narrative, one with different temporal, spatial, or personal deictic anchoring.

As we begin to look at stories in some detail a bit further on, it will become increasingly clear that speakers adhere very consistently to the narrative conventions outlined here. There is nothing structurally "casual" about an everyday story. Upon close examination, a story told in a conversation reveals itself to be as formally constructed as any carefully worked out acknowledged piece of literary verbal art. Just as a conventional novelist will take pains to make clear where a story took place geographically and temporally, who was involved, and what important events had happened previous to the beginning of the story he wants to tell, a conversational storyteller telling a casual friend what went on the supermarket checkout line last Wednesday will supply enough relevant setting information to locate the story in time and space early on in the telling. Throughout the story, information important to understanding the state of affairs in the storyworld will be given at times appropriate to building and updating an adequate model of the changing world of the discourse.

To distinguish those propositions encoding states of affairs in a narrative world which are not punctual events on the main time line from those events which are, we shall refer to the state and non-main line events collectively as *durative-descriptive propositions*. These are encoded in *durative-descriptive clauses*. Descriptions of characters, settings, and motivations are durative-descriptive, along with habitual, iterative, or noninstantaneous actions and events which are semantically interpreted to be off the main time line, in flash sequences, for example. In stories and reports, the narrative genres discussed in this study, durative-descriptive clauses often predominate.

2.3 STORIES: SPECIFIC PAST TIME NARRATIVES WITH A POINT

Linguistic texts are produced to accomplish communicative aims. *Stories* are told to make a point, to transmit a message—often some sort of moral evaluation or implied critical judgment—about the world the teller shares with other people. Exactly what telling a story involves in this respect, can be gotten at somewhat indirectly by considering the *report,* often linguistically identical to the story in terms of event and state information, but differing dramatically in impact. Any parent who has ever received a dreary "report" of the day's happenings instead of a "story" in response to a cheery "Well, dear, what happened in school today?" will testify to the difference.

A report, unlike a story, is most typically elicited by the recipient—like the hapless parent in the example above—or in response to circumstances which require an accounting of what went on. The context of reporting supplies a framework in which the relevance of the states and events reported can be ascertained. In fact, the recipient may even assign relevance to very specific pieces of information whose importance escapes the narrator. (For example, in reports told by witnesses to the police.) The burden of assigning differential weighting to the various narrated propositions thus falls to the receiver of the report. The reporter himself may implicitly tell the elicitor, "O.K., you wanted to know. *You* figure out why I should have told you all this." In a story, however, key events bring about changes in the storyworld which are relevant to the point which is being made, while less important events move people and objects about and mark the passage of time necessary to a narrative. Likewise, some crucial durative-descriptive information communicates those states of affairs which are altered by the key events. Other durative-descriptive propositions are properly considered "background" information. Tellers, therefore, *evaluate* the key events most highly in order to distinguish them from the other less important instantaneous main time line events. Crucial durative-descriptive information is likewise highlighted by the teller in the telling to emphasize the most important non-event story propositions. Evaluation allows the story recipients to build up a model of the relevant information in the text which matches the teller's intentions as signalled by the manner in which the information about the storyworld is communicated.

2.3.1 "EVALUATION" IN CONVERSATIONAL STORIES

In storytelling, the burden of making the relevance of the telling clear falls on the narrator. Insofar as they share a common world view, the narrator and intended story recipients have similar basic understandings of people, objects, and occurrences—the material world, in short, and the intricate complex of values and beliefs which are used to assign meaning to the goings-on in that world and to make sense of experience. The narrator relies upon this common understanding to constrain the interlocutors to infer the same point from the goings on in the storyworld which he himself infers. Although the narrator may make the message of the story explicit in an introductory comment or concluding remark—the juxtaposition of events and states which make up the telling must be encoded so that the message is clear even without those added remarks.

Stories are highly complex discourses, however, and not all the propositions about the storyworld are equally important to the point which the story is being told to illustrate. In essence, a story consists of events which took place in particular circumstances, involved particular characters, and gave rise to states of affairs which contrast in some way with the situation obtaining in the storyworld at the beginning of the story. Every world is composed of innumerable states of affairs, and a storyworld is no different. However, only a few of these are significant to the point being made in a given telling and, therefore, only the events which cause alterations in those states bring about a contrasting state which is "meaningful." In telling a story, the narrator has two tasks: to give enough detail so that interlocutors understand the nature of the change brought about, and to differentiate among the various events and states which are used to tell the story so that it is clear to the interlocutors precisely which complex of circumstances and events should be used to infer the point being made. Highlighting the most important information in the story at the expense of less important information is accomplished by according each proposition a more or less distinctive form of encoding; the more distinct the encoding, the more the information encoded stands out from the rest of the text and the better it is remembered. Put most generally, the more salient the form of encoding, the more salient the information encoded is assumed to be.

Evaluation, as this process of assigning prominence is called, is accomplished by encoding the information to be accorded increased weight in a way which departs from the local norm of the text. In spoken language, speakers signal salience by using any one of a fairly large battery of conventional linguistic and paralinguistic *evaluative devices* drawn from every level of linguistic structure (Labov, 1972). It should be borne in mind, however, that there are no "absolute" evaluative devices; any device available for evaluation can be used nonevaluatively as well or can be so over-used that it becomes a textual norm.

Phonologically, a speaker may pronounce a word in a distinctive way, accentuate an odd syllable, or use a distinctive dialectal sound quality. Changes in stress and volume are also available to mark prominence as well as onomatopoeia, rhyme, and nonlinguistic noises. Lexically, a speaker may choose a word from a different register from the text norm—perhaps using a colloquial word in a formal text or vice–versa. "Loaded" words may be used, words rich in connotations. Profanity, foreign words and precise use of relatively infrequent words also can be used to draw attention to the proposition so encoded.

Syntactically, as Labov (1972) has shown, a multitude of resources are available, including modification, the use of comparators, superlatives, and negative sentences (which evaluate what *was* the state of affairs in the storyworld by making explicit what was not the case). Modal operators and adverbials which shift the point of view from one frame of reference to another can also be evaluative, as can other types of elaboration and specification phenomena which highlight some aspect of the discourse world by giving a good deal of information about it. Any marked change in syntactic complexity calls attention to itself whether by a shift into a simple sentence from a stretch of highly attenuated sentences or vice versa. In stories, the first event after a string of durative-descriptive clauses demands special attention, as does the first compound-complex sentence after a number of relatively short uncomplicated sentences.

At the discourse level, a wide variety of devices are available; repetition, reported speech or thought, flashbacks or flashaheads which delay the action, and explicit meta-comments as well as "clustering" a number of events at the "peak" of the story are common in many narrative traditions around the world (Longacre, 1976). While "reported speech and thought" is often an important discourse level evaluative device, it should be pointed out that direct and indirect discourse only function evaluatively where not normative. In a "he said/she said" story told in dialogue, reported speech is the encoding norm and often important information in these stories will be encoded in nondialogic form.

The use of evaluation must be highly monitored and, it is not too far–fetched to say, orchestrated by the teller. The degree of salience accorded any proposition by use of any evaluative device or combination of devices depends on the power of the device or set of devices at that specific moment in the telling. If a device has been heavily used earlier, for example, it is no longer so "surprising" or arresting—a change in effectiveness analogous to the functioning of much "forte" in music. Exactly as forte becomes the "normal" volume and a change to "piano" is strongly perceived, a shift from a heavily used device, such as increased volume or heavy modification, to one which has not been used frequently in that telling so far, will function to bring the material so evaluated into sharper focus.

In addition to monitoring the use of evaluative devices themselves, the narrator must also monitor the relative amount of evaluation accorded the many propositions. In order to assure each proposition the amount of foregrounding it should have, the teller must keep track of how much evaluation each proposition was accorded earlier in the telling. If the narrator used evaluation freely in previous clauses, he must increase the evaluation—either in numbers of evaluators or distinctiveness (or a combination of both)—in marking subsequent propositions he finds more important.

Evaluation of information encoded in one clause by devices realized in other clauses—whether with scope inside the storyworld or beyond it—is called *deictic evaluation* to contrast it with *contential evaluation* in which the evaluating device and evaluated information are within the same clause. Along with comments about the story, there are a number of other commonly used deictic devices including elaboration in later clauses on information presented earlier, generalization from one instance to the general case, flash sequences which give explanatory information, and, often, reported speech. (Except in a story in which someone acquires the power of speech, speaking in and of itself is not usually significant. What is said may be significant or may point beyond to some other aspect of the storyworld indicated by the remark.) Repetition is the purest deictic device—what is evaluated achieves prominence by the fact of the repetition which does not, in itself, have any embodiment.[1]

The same clause may contain evaluative structures functioning both deictically and contentially; some information in the clause itself may be highlighted by one or more

---

[1]Contentially evaluated propositions are themselves encoded in a distinctive manner within the clause. Most of the linguistic devices discussed earlier can be used for contential evaluation. Again, it must be emphasized that evaluation is not a property of any given linguistic or paralinguistic structure per se. Evaluation functions by departing from the locally established norm of the text—it is a use to which any linguistic structure can be put and is not in itself a property of any structure. Deictic and contential evaluation, similarly, may be used simultaneously by a speaker in constructing a given clause. To be "contentially" or "deictically" evaluative is not a property of specific devices but depend upon the use to which the device is put in the discourse.

devices within the clause, while others point beyond the confines of the clause to evaluate other information elsewhere in the text. Of course, information in that same clause may itself be evaluated by devices elsewhere in the text. One very common occurrence of this multiple evaluative functioning is found in clauses encoding repeated information. While repetition is a deictic evaluator, as has been pointed out, what is repeated may be contentially evaluated as well.

In most storytelling traditions, more than one device is at work in a story text and more than one piece of information is highlighted by a mixture of deictic and contential evaluators. Typically, as Longacre (1976) has pointed out, important information is evaluated by a number of devices acting in concert; devices as well as events cluster at the peak of the action. Particularly arresting evaluators involving a marked degree of narrator participation are common in American oral storytelling to mark the most significant storyworld propositions (Eisner, 1976). External commentary, expressive phonology, and direct appeals to the story recipients collapse the NOW of the storyworld with the RIGHT NOW of the narration and make the reported events and states immediate and part of the ongoing interaction. Often these evaluative devices are encoded in clauses which must be interpreted as having scope outside the storyworld. The deictic devices point in from beyond the frame of the story—usually from the perspective of the embedding talk in conversational storytelling—at the goings on inside the storyworld. Normally, both some events on the main time line ("story events") and some durative-descriptive information will be heavily evaluated by the teller. Since the most important (i.e., foregrounded) non-event states of affairs in a Storyworld are changed significantly by the most highly evaluated events, the "core plot" of a story can be captured by attending carefully to evaluation.

The linguistic structure of the text itself, reveals what is most relevant to the teller in a specific telling (unless, as may happen, of course, a teller manipulates these conventions for his own strategic purposes—as happens in mystery stories for example). Therefore, starting from the information about story structure and the theoretical assumptions about the nature of stories outlined here, it is possible to construct a paraphrase of the telling, an *Adequate Paraphrase,* using only the most heavily evaluated main line story events (*key events*) and the most heavily evaluated durative descriptive information (*crucial contextualizing information* or *CCI*). The Adequate Paraphrase, composed entirely of the elements singled out by the teller for special emphasis, eliminates all incidental propositions. Since a very different story would result if any of the highly evaluated propositions which interact to create the story's problems and resolutions were omitted or overshadowed by other information in a subsequent telling, the Adequate Paraphrase seems to come close to a reasonable representation of the given telling of a story.

2.4 CONSTRUCTING AN ADEQUATE-PARAPHRASE FOR A STORY

In order to construct an Adequate Paraphrase (A.P.), it is necessary to attend very closely to the encoding details of the many clauses which constitute the storytelling text. After a list of main line event and durative-descriptive propositions has been assembled, the weighting accorded each proposition by the evaluative meta-structure can be assessed. Eventually an Adequate Paraphrase can be assembled from the Key Events and Crucial Contextualizing Information. The paraphrase maintains the order which the propositions have in the source text.

This procedure, summarized in detail in Chart 1, entitled "To Construct an Adequate Paraphrase from a Story Text" (pp. 19–20) has six main parts:

1. Division of the story into individual clauses or independent utterances
2. Listing Main Line Story Event Clauses and Durative-Descriptive Clauses and Non-Storyworld Clauses
3. Preparing lists of the corresponding propositions
4. Analyzing the functioning of the evaluative meta-structure
5. Roughly calculating the amount of evaluation accorded each storyworld proposition
6. Combining the most heavily evaluated Story Event and Durative-Descriptive Propositions into a stylistically acceptable Adequate Paraphrase which preserves the ordering of clauses.

The first step, which calls for dividing the text of the telling into individual clauses or "independent utterances" sounds both simple to do and relatively unimportant. However, it is, in fact, neither, but rather is the cornerstone of the entire enterprise and presents its own, not insubstantial, difficulties. Under the rubric "independent utterances" are included minimal responses, such as "yes" and "no," "well," "but," "so" and other discourse particles (whose functioning is a field of study in itself); as well as "you know," "man," and other parentheticals; exclamations; and unfinished phrases which surface in texts in hesitations, repetitions, false starts, and other phenomena. This assorted linguistic material has in common with fully formed main and subordinate clauses and nonclausal "complete thoughts" its unitary nature. While in an ideal text the chunking might well be into clauses because clauses may encode full propositions, all of the other structures which occur in a real text must be accommodated as well. Each of these "unitary" words, phrases, or near-linguistic utterances may function in the text either to provide fragmentary propositional information about the storyworld or the speaker's attitude towards his material. Thus, none can be discarded, but each item should be isolated, no less rigorously than the well-formed clauses themselves, so that its functioning in the text can be evaluated.

The text must be neatly chunked, in order to divide the various information it encodes into storyworld and non-storyworld *propositions*. Among storyworld propositions, the Main Line Story Events must be separated from the Durative-Descriptive Propositions by examining each clause (or part) individually and making a judgment about its temporal interpretation. Those clauses which are syntactically main clauses, semantically event clauses, and which should be interpreted as events on the main time line of the story, make up the list of Main Line Story Event Clauses. Other storyworld clauses, (including those which are events displaced temporally because they are included in extended explanations or answers to questions), make up the list of Durative-Descriptive Clauses. Non-Storyworld Clauses are placed on a separate list.[2]

The propositions are listed in the order in which they occur in the source text. The temporal ordering of the source text is thus preserved. In the case of reported speech, what was said is represented as subordinate to a matrix verb of saying. If the reported speech is direct discourse, the verb of the matrix clause is an event, while what is said is not. Full references are substituted for anaphoric or deictic expressions and, as far as possible, the clause is normalized into an affirmative statement with the scopes of negatives and other modals relatively clear.

Translating encoding clauses into their propositional form, is, therefore, relatively straightforward. As a general rule, the need to make many inferences at this point in the procedure is limited. (Inferences from the Paraphrase to the cultural presuppositions which underlie the "plots" is the work of understanding the Adequate Paraphrases themselves, which will be addressed in detail later on in this study.) However, once the lists of propositions have been assembled and attention is turned to establishing the operation of evaluation in a given story, it may be necessary to make simple inferences (using "world knowledge") from the explicitly stated information to the implied results of actions or other easily made associations. This permits important textual redundancies to emerge which might otherwise remain obscure. (It might well turn out that these redundancies would not be apparent to someone who was not a competent in a given culture.)

What must always be done, however, in order to build an Adequate Paraphrase is a careful analysis of the details of encoding the various Story Event and Durative-Descriptive Propositions. Changes in encoding norms must be carefully considered and exactly what information is being highlighted ascertained. Contential evaluators for each clause are often relatively easy to identify, while deictic evaluation, since it operates across the text, is often more difficult. Flashbacks and flashaheads often act as both contential and deictic evaluators, delaying the action, giving important contextualizing information, and so forth; along with repeated and redundant elements, they must be looked at very carefully. As a final step in analyzing the text for

---

[2]It is very important to separate out the non-storyworld propositions from storyworld events and states. Proceeding through the text on a clause-by-clause basis is the only way to make sure that the temporal interpretation of each clause is assessed correctly. This assures that the non-storyworld talk is seen to be distinct from storyworld events and states, permitting an analyst to "find the story in all the talk"—a nontrivial problem for those working with conversational stories of the sort we shall be examining in the next chapter.

[3]In Richard Hughes' novel, *A High Wind in Jamaica*, for example, the Key Event—a child falling to his death—is encoded in a simple, otherwise unevaluated event clause. Although the results of the death as well as many of the other circumstances in the novel are very elaborately described, the fall is as silent and unnoticed in the text as it was in the story. (Such deceptive negative evaluating is seldom found in everyday storytelling except by tellers skillful in building mysteries and handling suspense and the unexpected. However, we shall encounter some equally sophisticated evaluation and nonevaluation in the stories in the next chapter.)

evaluation, the non-storyworld comments should be examined for deictic reference to material inside the storyworld.

Once all of this has been done, one can get a rough idea of the relative amount of prominence accorded each proposition by adding up the number of evaluators attached to each. In many cases, evaluators which show a marked degree of narrator involvement (acting out part of the story, increased gesticulation, screaming, or "dramatic whispers") should be given more weight than a simple elaborating detail. Sometimes an apparent evaluative device will, upon further reflection, appear to have lost most of its force through overuse. The information so encoded may thus be somewhat less highlighted than at first glance. Often at this point, too, redundancy of information will become increasingly obvious and the evaluative force of *nonelaboration* in a text of otherwise highly modified details may be surprisingly effective.[3]

Once all of this preparatory work has been done, the Adequate Paraphrase can be assembled from the most highly evaluated Story Event and Durative-Descriptive Propositions. These are then combined into a mini-text, small stylistic adjustments can be made, and the Paraphrase is complete. (The exact degree of detail included in the Paraphrase may vary depending on the use to which it is to be put. If only the most highly evaluated propositions are included, it will necessarily be sparser than if all heavily evaluated propositions are included. (See Polanyi [1981] for a discussion of this point.)

CHART 1
To Construct an Adequate Paraphrase from a Story Text

---

1. Divide up the text into clauses.
2. Separate out any clauses whose scope lies entirely outside the storyworld. Consider the content of these clauses when assessing evaluation (Step 9c)
3. Note which storyworld clauses are main clauses and which are syntactically subordinate clauses.
4. Examine the verb of each main clause.
5. List as Main Story Line Events only those main clauses which fulfill all event criteria (active, affirmative, punctual, noniterative, completive) and which are in the simple past (or historical present) tense. Exclude any event clauses which do not form part of the main time line (flashed clauses, for example).
6. List as Event Propositions the propositional content of the Main Line Story Event clauses.
7. List as Durative-Descriptive all Nonevent storyworld clauses.
8. List as Durative-Descriptive Propositions the propositional content of the Durative-Descriptive clauses.
9. Consider carefully how each Storyworld Proposition is encoded.
    a. Examine the text in sections of a few clauses, looking for distinctive encodings—encodings which stand out because they depart noticeably from the locally established encoding norm. Consider such departures (contentially or deictically) evaluative.
    b. Examine the text globally. Look for repetitions of words, phrases, clauses, redundancy of propositional content, extensive details, delays in giving expected information, flash sequences,

(continued)

CHART 1 (*Continued*)

conversational interludes dealing with the storyworld, and so on. Consider such discourse-level phenomena (deictically) evaluative.

c. Consider the nonstoryworld clauses (including para-linguistic phenomena such as laughter and kinesic phenomena such as marked gesturing). Notice any reference or commentary on Storyworld propositions. Consider such discourse-level phenomena (deictically) evaluative.

10. Keep a rough accounting of how much evaluation each Storyworld Proposition is accorded.

11. List those Main Line Story Event Propositions which were most heavily evaluated in the order in which they occurred in the source text.

12. List those Durative-Descriptive Propositions which received most evaluation in the order in which they occurred in the source text.

13. Combine the Key Events (from 11) and the Crucial Contextualizing Information (from 12) in the order in which they occurred in the source text.

14. Make minor syntactic and stylistic changes in the text resulting from Step 13 so that the resulting paraphrase is easily understandable. (This may include combining information with logical connectives, subordinating one proposition to another, eliminating multiple definite descriptors by using pronouns, and so on.)

2.5 "THE BADDEST GIRL IN THE NEIGHBORHOOD"

So far, this discussion has been quite theoretical. Now it is time to see exactly what happens when this procedure is tried out on a real story. The story which will be used was collected by Labov and Waletzky in answer to the question, "What was the most important fight that you remember, one that sticks in your mind?" I have named the story "The Baddest Girl in the Neighborhood" in order to identify it easily. The analysis which is presented below, which eventually results in an Adequate Paraphrase of this story, partially overlaps with the analysis done by Labov of the same story and presented in his 1972 paper, "The Transformation of Experience in Narrative Syntax." It is fitting, that his analysis be taken up and enlarged in this book because much of the work on story structure presented thus far in this chapter can be traced more or less directly to his insights about the functioning of oral narrative (Labov and Waletzky, 1967; Labov, 1972).

(Rather than repeat large portions of "The Baddest Girl in the Neighborhood" frequently, the text given below is already divided into clauses. This division does not correspond to the one given by Labov [1972, p. 383] in which nonstoryworld clauses are included in with the clause to which they seem to belong and the text of reported speech is listed together with the reporting clause. The Durative-Descriptive Clauses, which make up the bulk of the story, are marked here with a "D". All storyworld main clauses, are marked with an asterisk to make it easier to identify those clauses which may be Main Line Story Event Clauses.)

"THE BADDEST GIRL IN THE NEIGHBORHOOD"

D * 1. (Well) one of the most important fights I had was with a girl.
    2. I think
D * 3. And she was the baddest girl, the baddest girl in the neighborhood
D   4. If you didn't bring her candy to school
D * 5. She would punch you in the mouth.
D * 6. And you had to kiss her
D   7. when she'd tell you
D * 8. This girl was only 12 years old
    9. man
D *10. but she was a killer
D *11. She didn't take no junk
D *12. She whupped all her brothers
  *13. And I came to school one day
D *14. And I didn't have no money
D *15. My ma wouldn't give me no money
D *16. And I played hookies one day
D *17. (She) put something on me
D *18. I played hookies
  19. man
D *20. (so) I said
D 21. you know
D 22. "I'm not gonna play hookies no more
D 23. cause I don't wanna get a whuppin'"
  *24. So I go to school
  *25. and this girl says
D 26. "Where's the candy?"
  *27. I said
D 28. "I don't have it"
  *29. She says
D 30. powww!
  *31. (so) I says to myself
D 32. "There's gonna be times
D 33. my mother won't give me money
D 34. because (we're) a poor family
D 35. And I can't take all of this.
  36. you know
D 37. everytime she don't give me any money."
  *38. (So) I say
D 39. ("Well), I just gotta fight this girl
D 40. She gonna hafta whup me.
D 41. I hope she don't whup me."
  *42. And I hit the girl

D   43. powww!
  *44. and I put something on it.
D   45. I win the fight.[4]

Once the text has been listed, it is not difficult to go through it clause by clause and separate out the non-storyworld clauses which are not numerous, in any case, in this story:

Non-Storyworld Clauses

  2. I think
  9. man
19. man
21. you know
36. you know

The Story Event Clauses are also relatively simple to identify. However, it is necessary to watch carefully for the flashback interlude in which the narrator tells about his earlier dismal experience with playing hooky. The events in the flashback should not be included in with the Story Event Clauses since they are not on the main story line.

Story Event Clauses[5]

13. I came to school one day
24. So I go to school [= 13]
25. <u>and this girl says</u> "Where's the candy."
27. <u>I said</u> "I don't have it."
29. <u>She says</u>: powww!
31. <u>So I says to myself</u> "There's gonna be times my mother won't give me money because (we're) a poor family. And I can't take all of this everytime she don't give me any money."
37. <u>So I say</u> "Well, I just gotta fight this girl. She gonna hafta whup me. I hope she don't whup me."
42. And I hit the girl.

---

[4]There is some question concerning the classification of Clause 45, which can be used to illustrate the profound problems raised by the State/Event distinction. I am arguing here that "I win the fight" is a state because it expresses the initiating of the state resulting from having had the fight—as does the sentence "The Allies won the war." It is possible, however, to consider that the narrator won the fight at one discrete moment. Labov apparently did so when he included this clause in his list of "narrative clauses" [equivalent to the Mainline Story Event Clauses in our terminology] (p. 384). It may be significant that this problem arose in relation to a clause found at the *end* of a discrete segment of the talk—in this case at the end of the telling as we have it recorded. The difficulties make no deeply significant difference to our analysis, in any case, since the clause is unevaluated.

[5]Event clause underlined.

The Main Line Story Event Propositions and Durative-Descriptive Propositions are listed below. To avoid confusion, the clause numbers from the original listing of the story have been retained: i.e. "Story Event Proposition 13/24" corresponds to the propositional content of clauses 13 and 24. (The matrix event clause of reported speech is underlined.)

Mainline Story Event Propositions

13/24. The narrator went to school
   25. The Baddest Girl asked for candy.
   27. The narrator said he had none.
   29. The Baddest Girl said Powww!
   31. The narrator said to himself that he could not take all this abuse everytime his mother did not give him money which she will not do because they are a poor family.
   37. The narrator said (to himself) that he must fight the Baddest Girl and she would have to whup him although he hoped she would not (be able to?).
42/44. The narrator hit the Baddest Girl (hard).

The Durative-Descriptive Propositions create a somewhat longer list. (The underlined portion of some propositions is the durative-descriptive reported speech governed by Story Events which are not underlined. If the reporting clause is in a flashback and also durative-descriptive nothing in that proposition is underlined.)

Durative-Descriptive Propositions

   1. The narrator had a very important fight with a girl.
   2. The girl was the baddest girl in the neighborhood.
   3. The girl made people bring her candy.
   4. The girl punched people in the mouth.
   5. The girl made people kiss her.
   6. The girl would tell people to kiss her.
   8. The girl was only 12 years old.
  10. The girl was a killer.
  11. The girl didn't take junk.
  12. The girl whupped all her brothers.
  14. The narrator had no money one day.
  15. The narrator's mother wouldn't give him money.
16/18. The narrator had once played hookies.
  17. The narrator's mother beat him for playing hookies.
  22. That he would not play hookies any more was said by the narrator.
  23. That he did not want to get a whuppin' for playing hookies was said by the narrator.
  26. That she wanted to know where the candy was was asked by the girl.
  27. That he didn't have any candy was said by the narrator

30. <u>powww</u>! was "said" by the girl.
31. <u>That there would be times</u> was said by the narrator to himself.
33/37. <u>That his mother would not give him money at all times</u> was said by the narrator to himself.
34. <u>That they were a poor family</u> was said by the narrator to himself.
35. <u>That he could not take all of this</u> (<u>bullying</u>) was said by the narrator to himself.
39. <u>That he would have to fight the girl</u> was said by the narrator to himself.
40. <u>That she would have to whup him</u>, was said to the narrator to himself.
41. <u>That he hoped that she didn't whup him</u> was said to the narrator by himself.
45. The narrator won the fight.

Once the Story Event Propositions and the Durative-Descriptive Propositions have been identified, the next steps require extensive analysis of the evaluation structure of the story text. Since this is quite tedious to follow step by step, this detailed information has been put together in Chart 2, "Summary of Analysis of 'The Baddest Girl in the Neighborhood'". (The chart has six columns. Each clause of the story is analyzed consecutively, each on its own line. The first columns, headed "Clause number" and "Clause", respectively, are self-explanatory. The third column, "Story Event (E) or Durative Descriptive (D)" indicates whether a storyworld clause is a Main Line Event Clause ("E") or a Durative-Descriptive Clause ("D"). If the clause is not a storyworld clause, it is marked "N.S." for Non–Storyworld. In the fourth and fifth column, the propositional content of the clause is given if it is evaluated at all. If it was left evaluated in the telling, these columns will both be left blank. The fourth column, "Proposition + Contential Evaluators," lists the proposition and any contential evaluators found within the clause which evaluate it. In the fifth column, "Proposition + Deictic Evaluators," is found the proposition (or abbreviated version of it if it was given in full in column 4) and details of deictic evaluators found elsewhere, which act to evaluate it. The clause in which those deictic evaluators occur is also listed. In the last column, headed "Other Clauses Evaluated by this Clause," the deictic functioning of the clause under consideration is specified with the clause(s) which it evaluates and the method of evaluation.[6])

Although "The Baddest Girl in the Neighborhood" was elicited in answer to a question (*"What was the most important fight that you remember? One that sticks in your mind?"*), it contains a great many evaluative devices acting on a number of different storyworld propositions to make clear that the fight described can qualify as an "important" one worth telling about. These range from expressive phonology (*"Powww!"*) and sentence and discourse level devices which provide elaboration, specification, and generalization of propositions to external comments on states of affairs in the narrative world (*"you know"*, *"man"*, *"I think"*). Of the many propositions evaluated by at least one evaluative device, many function deictically to evaluate

---

[6]The chart for "Eating on the New York Thruway" [See pp. 41–43 below] is considerably simpler than this one because it is based on propositions rather than clauses. It seemed useful to give the full analysis from clauses to Adequate Paraphrase at least once.

information elsewhere in the text. The most heavily evaluated Durative-Descriptive Propositions ("*The girl was the baddest girl in the neighborhood.*" [Proposition 21]) and ("*That the narrator was poor*" [inferred from combining explicit propositions 14/15/33–37/34]) and ("*That he would no longer be bullied*" [Proposition 35]) and the Key Event ("*The narrator hit the girl*" [Proposition 42/44]) are each evaluated both contentially and deictically. I will assess each of these most important propositions individually. Readers are encouraged to consult the Summary Chart to see the specific details.

The badness of the girl is explained at great length at the beginning of the story. Ten of the first twelve clauses concern the girl's toughness, one fifth of the total clauses in the whole telling. This girl was *bad;* she would punch people if they did not give her candy. She was a twelve year old "*killer*" (marked word choice) who forced people to kiss her and would beat up her own brothers. This specification is important to emphasize the girl's character and to provide motivation for the narrator to hit her back. She was a girl, and boys in our society do not beat up girls without very good reason if they wish to appear proper persons—let alone emerge as champions of the poor and oppressed.

The narrator's poverty is another highly evaluated state of affairs in the storyworld. The information to infer this proposition is found in several individual propositions and the redundant encoding of the narrator coupled with "*no money*" is a very strong evaluator here. It is explained that the narrator had no money (Proposition 14), why he had no money (Proposition 15), and that he might often (Proposition 31) have no money because his mother would not give him any (Propositions 33/37). This last is not because his mother lacks generosity, but because hers was a poor family. (Proposition 34). The information about the narrator's poverty was evaluated by its encoding in direct thought.

The narrator's impecunious state leads to his decision; he will no longer be bullied. The narrator's analysis of his situation and his generalization from the specific instance to the general case is encoded in direct thought, a shift from the direct speech of previous clauses, and marks a change in narrative perspective from that of the external removed observer to participant in the character's thought processes. His decision to fight back is marked by the presence of the narrator and his appeal to the story recipients with "*you know*" (Clause 36) in addition to the anaphoric statement "*I can't take all of this*", *Which* chunks the preceding action as one unit and tenders an implicit judgment on it—it is intolerable. The result of this analysis, then, is his explicit decision to fight the girl and stand up for his rights, culminating in the Key Event (hitting the girl) which is itself evaluated by onomatopoeia and specification of manner in subsequent clauses as well as the contential evaluation of the short non-speech, very decisive, event clause ("*I hit the girl*"). This is the first such clause (and only such clause, it will turn out) in the story which ends abruptly with the event clause, "*I win the fight*" and gives the result of the action.

A summary of the story which would capture the essence of the most highly evaluated propositions would include the following information:

1. The girl was the baddest girl in the neighborhood.
2. The narrator had no money.
3. The narrator could not tolerate being bullied (because he had no money).
4. The narrator hit the girl.

An Adequate Paraphrase of the story could thus be:

> The narrator hit "the baddest girl in the neighborhood" because he could not tolerate being bullied for having no money.

This strips the telling of its excitement, of its pathos, of its art, but preserves the information which we would need to ask a question about the story which would show real understanding of what had gone on. On the basis of such a paraphrase, we would be able to tell a "topically coherent" next story by building that next story around "fighting," "baddest girls," or "refusing to be bullied." A story built around "going to school" or "playing hooky" would need more introductory comment to establish why it was told.

If one were to hear a telling on another occasion which purported to be the "same story" as "The Baddest Girl in the Neighborhood" and the narrator left out the location of the confrontation or the fact that his mother had once beaten him for playing hooky, one would have no serious difficulty in judging the two tellings to be "essentially" the same. The story is not really "about" hooky and we have very little impression of where the fight took place. On the other hand, if the narrator left out the fact that the girl was a bully we would think poorly rather than well of the narrator for fighting the girl. He would emerge as a bully himself, beating up people (assumed to be) weaker than himself. If his poverty were eliminated, we would also lose the point of this story. This is not really about a "fight", per se, nor is it really about "fighting girls." In this telling of these events, the narrator stands up for his rights against a stronger force. It is a story of courage. We know which culturally significant inferences to draw from the conjunction of poverty—stronger forces—deciding to fight. For Americans, it is a standard plot but merely because it is essentially stereotypic, it is none the weaker. Rather it is stronger. The presupposed "facts of life" which give this story much of its impact will be explored in Chapter Four following the discussion of conversational story structures in the next chapter.

CHART 2
Evaluation in "The Baddest Girl in the Neighborhood"

Clause Number	Clause	Story Event (E) or Durative Descriptive (D)	Proposition + Contential Evaluators	Proposition + Deictic Evaluators	Other Clauses Evaluated by this Clause
1.	(Well,) one was with a girl	D		This fight most important (Clause 2)	
2.	I think	N.S.			External comment (Clause 1)
3.	And she was the baddest girl in the neighborhood	D	The girl was the worst girl in the neighborhood. (repetition of superlative)	Girl the worst girl in neighborhood. Specification (Clauses 4–9; 11–12) by external comment (Clause 10)	
4.	If you didn't bring her candy to school	D			Negative conditional (Clause 3)
5.	She would punch you in the mouth	D			Universal result (Clause 3) $detail_1$
6.	And you had to kiss her	D			Universal imperative (Clause 3) $detail_2$
7.	when she'd tell you	D			Universal conditional (Clause 3)
8.	This girl was only about 12 years old	D	The girl was 12 years old ("only about"—modification)		Charaterization (Clause 3) $detail_3$
9.	man	N.S.			external exclamation (Clause $8/9 = 3$)
10.	but she was a killer	D	The girl was a killer = very bad. ("killer"-loaded word)	Girl a young killer: Contrast (Clause 8)	Loaded characterization (Clause 3) $detail_4$
11.	She didn't take no junk	D	The girl did not tolerate what she did not like (?) (negative statement)		Negative characterization (Clause 3) $detail_5$

(continued)

27

CHART 2 (*Continued*)

Clause Number	Clause	Story Event (E) or Durative Descriptive (D)	Proposition + Contential Evaluators	Proposition + Deictic Evaluators	Other Clauses Evaluated by this Clause
12.	She whupped all her brothers	D	The girl beat up her brothers [won fights with boys = strong]		Characterization (Clause 3) detail$_6$
13.	And I came to school one day	E			
14.	And I didn't have no money	D	Narrator had no money. (Negative proposition)	Narrator had no money. Repeated specification (Clause 15,33,37)	
15.	My ma wouldn't give me no money	D	Mother gave narrator no money. (Negative proposition)		Specification (Clause 14) detail$_1$
16.	And I played hookies one day	D	Narrator had played hooky. (Repetition)	Narrator had once played hooky. Repetition (Clause 18) external comment (Clause 19)	
17.	She put something on me	D			
18.	I played hookies	D		Narrator had played hooky. External comment (Clause 19)	
19.	man	N.S.			External comment (Clause 18)
20.	(So) I said	D			Direct Discourse (Clause 22)
21.	You know	N.S.			External comment (Clause 22)
22.	"I'm not gonna play hookies no more	D	Narrator will not play hooky [i.e. Narrator will go to school] (Direct discourse)	Narrator will not play hooky. External comment (Clause21) Specification (Clause 23)	

28

23.	D	cause I don't wanna get a whuppin'"	Narrator does not want to be whipped. (Direct discourse; negative proposition)		Specification (Clause 22) detail₁
24.	E(=13)	(So) I go to school			Direct discourse (Clause 26)
25.	E	and this girl says			
26.	D	"Where's the candy?"	Girl asks for candy.(Direct discourse)		Direct discourse (Clause 26)
27.	E	I said	Narrator has no candy. (Negative proposition. Direct discourse.)		
28.	D	"I don't have it"			
29.	E	She says			Action encoded as direct discourse (Clause 30)
30.	D	powww!	Narrator hit by baddest girl. (Action encoded as direct discourse; onomatopoeia.		
31.	E	(So) I says to myself			Direct discourse (Clause 32–37)
32.	D	"There's gonna be times			
33.	D	my mother won't give me money	Mother won't give money [=Narrator has no money] (Hypothetical; negative)	Mother won't give money [=Narrator has no money] Specification (Clause 34)	Specification (Clause 33) Reference (Clause 24–30)
34.	D	because [we're] a poor family			
35.	D	And I can't take all of this	Narrator cannot tolerate being bullied. (Negative proposition)		
36.	N.S.	you know	Presence of narrator.		External comment (Clauses 35;37)

(continued)

$detail_1$

CHART 2 (Continued)

Clause Number	Clause	Story Event (E) or Durative Descriptive (D)	Proposition + Contential Evaluators	Proposition + Deictic Evaluators	Other Clauses Evaluated by this Clause
37.	everytime she don't give me any money"	D	Mother doesn't give money [Narrator has no money] (Negative proposition; repetition)		Specification (Clause 35)
38.	(So) I say	E			Reported thought (Clause 39–41)
39.	"Well, I just gotta fight this girl.	D	Narrator must fight the baddest girl. (Necessity)		
40.	She gonna hafta whup me.	D	Baddest girl must beat narrator. [i.e. Narrator will fight baddest girl] (Future necessity)		
41.	I hope she don't whup me.	D	Narrator hopes girl doesn't beat him. (Negative hypothetical)		
42.	And I hit the girl	E	Narrator hit the baddest girl. (Short event sentence. First positive action by narrator. First non "housekeeping", non-reported discourse event.)	Narrator hit the baddest girl. Specification (Clauses 43–44) onomatopoeia (Clause 43)	
43.	powww!	D			Onomatopoeia (Clause 43)
44.	and I put something on it.	E [=42]	Narrator hit the baddest girl. (Repetition of action in clause 42)		Specification (Clause 43)
45.	I win the fight	ED			Result of action in Clause 42

3.

AMERICAN STORIES IN CONVERSATION

3.0 INTRODUCTION

Talk containing conversational stories is composed of a number of clauses only some of which have their reference inside a storyworld. A storytelling may be interrupted by talk which has nothing to do with the telling and may be resumed after the interruption is completed. The resumption itself, in these cases, is signalled by apologies and reinitiation markers ("So", "well", "where were we? Oh, yeah . . ."), none of which are of the storyworld. Even in a telling as seemingly unitary as "The Baddest Girl in the Neighborhood," some clauses may not encode states of affairs in the storyworld but express the teller's involvement with the social interaction in which the story is told. ("You know", "man", etc.) In this chapter, some of the constraints arising from the social context in which conversational storytelling takes place are considered. It should become clear that norms of proper social interaction generally obtaining in conversation are important forces in determining which storyworld propositions are included or emphasized in a given telling and precisely how they are encoded.

In order to understand these social constraints better, the discussion in the opening sections of this chapter relies heavily on important observations made by ethnomethodological conversational analysts and reported in Sacks (1970–71) and Jefferson (1979). Their aims do not coincide with the goals of the present enterprise. They are primarily interested in stories as "sequenced objects articulating with the context in which they are told" (Jefferson, 1979, p. 219) while this study concentrates on linguistic and cultural aspects of story structure. However, the two enterprises are compatible and even complementary. One must understand the social mechanisms through which individual stories are told in turn-by-turn talk in order to understand the surface structure of conversational stories. Yet, without an understanding of the internal linguistic and semantic structure of those stories, one could not hope to understand the abstract semantic objects realized in that talk.

3.1 CONSTRAINTS ON CONVERSATIONAL STORYTELLING

Generally speaking, conversations can be characterized as "democratic" because unlike speech events such as sermons, lectures, or interviews, in conversation all participants have equal access to the floor. Turn-taking occurs frequently and in an orderly manner. Considering the opportunities for more than one speaker to be talking at any given time, it is remarkable how seldom overlaps occur, even in a fast and furious discussion. Roughly speaking, clause boundaries mark a point of possible speaker change, and while speakers are under a very strong constraint to make their utterances somehow coherent with what has been going on immediately preceding their talking, this may be taken care of in the very opening parts of the turn, leaving the rest available to be directed as the speaker might wish. (See Sacks, Schegloff, and Jefferson, 1976 for a full discussion of turn-taking in conversation.)

Regular speaker change and the equal right of participants to determine the direction of talk are abandoned when one person decides to tell a story. Because stories are necessarily multi-clause turns (two events and a state clause are minimal) and those forced by the telling into the role of story recipients are not free to take a turn after any clause and use the information in that clause as a starting point for their own thoughts (Sacks, 1972). (Think of someone interrupting the narrator of "The Baddest Girl in the Neighborhood" in the middle of his telling to describe how he had once gone to school himself.) Rather, the story recipients must acknowledge that a story has been told by responding to it in some way which indicates acceptance of the fact that it was told and which demonstrates an understanding of what it was about. Should they not do so, they will be assumed to be ignoring the fact of the telling and displaying a degree of contempt for the story and thus for the teller.

Of necessity, the teller focuses attention on himself in telling a story. Not only is he the center of attention while claiming the floor for the duration of the extended turn, but he also makes explicit his judgment of what he believes the recipients would find worthwhile enough to justify relinquishing their rights to the floor. Therefore, by telling a story, the narrator exposes both an understanding of the recipients' interests and the degree of esteem in which he believes he is held. Because socially popular narrators command more attention than less well-regarded individuals (Eisner, 1974), storytellers whose stories "fall flat," suffer a loss of face and bring about an awkward social situation by making obvious their misjudgment of their status.

As Goffman (1967) and Brown and Levinson (1978) have shown, a loss of face for one member of an interaction is potentially threatening to the face of the other participants as well. The shame and embarrassment which would attend a failed storytelling may place the story recipients under an obligation to do something to save the teller's face and thus avoid a painful interlude. This obligation is thus a threat to *their* face, since failing to avoid unpleasantness indicates some degree of social incompetence. This ineptness escalates the teller's loss of face since had he not chosen to tell a story in the first place, the whole problem would not have arisen.

But speakers do take the risk of telling a story. After all, a successful storytelling may enhance the teller's face just as a storytelling failure diminishes it. In order to succeed in telling a conversational story there are a number of constraints which must be satisfied. We have dealt with a number of the more important linguistic and genre-specific constraints earlier:

1. To be a "story" at all, a linguistic text must encode a specific past time narrative description of the goings-on in a unique past time storyworld over a period of time. (A "narrative" description must include event propositions which encode instantaneous occurrences which took place at unique, discrete moments in the history of the storyworld.)
2. The story must have a "point." Cultural initiates must be able to infer meaning from the changes of state in the storyworld brought about by the key events.
3. Linguistically, a story must be structured conventionally. It must include both Main Line Event Clauses and contextualizing state clauses. Evaluative meta-information must be present so that story recipients can separate the most salient states and events from the others, thereby limiting the amount of inferencing necessary to find "the point."

In addition, conversational storytellers must take into account the circumstances obtaining in the interaction, which defines the context for the storytelling:

1. The "point" which can be inferred from the story must be relevant to the talk underway and seem to grow naturally out of that talk.
2. The story must be integrated smoothly into the preceding talk.
3. The teller must "recipient design" his story. What is said must be tailored to the specific people who are the story recipients.

When all of these constraints are met, one can begin to judge the story itself—was it "worth" telling, was it _really_ relevant, was it _really_ worth taking up a relatively large chunk of time in the conversation to tell this particular story exactly as it was told, was the "point" which the teller expected to be inferred _really_ illustrated by the goings-on in the storyworld? (In "Fainting on the Subway", discussed at the end of this chapter, there is an example of what may happen in the talk when a story as originally told does _not_ really seem to work precisely as the narrator had expected.)

3.2 STORIES IN CONVERSATION MUST BE "LOCALLY OCCASIONED" AND "RECIPIENT DESIGNED"

Carefully done, storytelling can be an effective and vivid way to explore a matter under discussion in some depth; poorly accomplished, however, telling a story in a conversation can be seen as self-indulgent digression, a blatant attempt to "grab the floor," change the subject, and put oneself forward. Therefore, a competent conversationalist does not begin a story at any random moment, but tries to build a bridge from a point being made in the general state of talk to some states of affairs in the storyworld which can be seen to relate in significant ways to what is being talked about.

Examination of conversational stories reveals that there is almost always some sort of talk preceding a storytelling (called "entrance talk" by Jefferson), which serves as a transition between the story proper and the embedding discussion. Entrance talk often includes a more or less explicit announcement that the teller intends to tell a story. This may be a conventional storytelling gambit such as "Did I ever tell you about the time when? . . ." This is followed by acceptance of the storytelling intent on the part of the recipients. In the entrance talk, the storyteller has a responsibility to make clear if he believes the story to be topically coherent with what has gone on before or if the storyworld propositions and point of the telling are not really relevant to the preceding talk. In the latter case, the storyteller has a positive obligation to "excuse" the fact that the story might be experienced as off the point. The excuse is often teamed with a justification of the importance of the story to the teller. In American conversational storytelling, complex entrance talk of the form "Oh! Wait a minute! That reminds me. I know it's off the point but I've got to tell you before I forget . . ." assures the recipients that their interests are being taken into account even as the talk is being routed, more or less brutally, into a storyworld.

Propositions which are properly assigned a semantic interpretation in a storyworld (along with the world of the telling, perhaps) mark the actual beginning of the story. Once the story is underway, the pressure to remain relevant to the immediate concerns of the story–recipients lessens. As Sacks (1971) and Jefferson (1979) have made clear, in storytelling, as in talk in general, speakers demonstrate "recipient design" in building their stories. Tellers may choose some aspects of the storyworld rather than others to dwell on in detail or may leave out information troubling to some recipients or problematic in the circumstances of one telling which might well be included another time. If some information must be included because it is central to understanding the point but is somehow distasteful to (some) recipients, the teller may apologize for having to mention it or may implicitly minimize it by hurrying through that part of the story, speaking rapidly, and with reduced volume.

Then, too, the storyteller must take into account the amount of information the story recipients have about various aspects of the story. A story which hinges on the foibles of a particular character will be told differently to someone who is familiar with the person and to someone who knows nothing about him. Failing to give enough explanation could bewilder some recipients who might then not understand the significance of the key events, for example, while giving too much information could insult and exasperate others. (See Schegloff [1971] for an explanation of similar recipient design problems in giving directions.)

The storyteller must make sure that the story recipients have enough information to "understand" the story because the recipients are constrained to exhibit understanding of the story both during the telling and immediately following in the "exit talk" which serves to re-establish the general state of talk. While story recipients must remain quiet and passive for the most part during the telling—they may not use a turn to start a new topic without "apologizing" for "interrupting", for example— there is a strong expectation that they will show their appreciation of the relevance of the storyworld propositions while the story is being told using nods, minimal responses, laughter, and comments to express interest, sympathy, or surprise. (Requests for clarification and specific questions about the storyworld are also appropriate means to display attention although such comments may be prefaced by apologies for not quite following.) Should the recipients fail to produce sufficient tokens of comprehension, the storyteller may interrupt the forward progress of the story and ask for confirmation that the recipients are, indeed, listening and understanding.

At the end of the story, it is incumbent on the story recipients to demonstrate understanding. After the story proper, there is conventionally exit talk of a couple of turns at least, which revolves around the story. At this time, the story recipients usually show whether the point of the story was taken to be comic or sad, about one event or another, or one circumstance or another. Often a recipient will ask a question about some key aspect of the story or people may laugh and repeat a phrase or two from a humorous story. The teller may also ask the recipients explicitly for a response or even elicit a story on a similar theme from them. By doing this, the teller simultaneously gives an interpretation of his own story and formally turns the floor over to the recipients. Since an absence of exit talk is, itself, a socially salient response indicating embarrassment, confusion, annoyance, lack of understanding, or low esteem for the teller, the teller who initiates the integration of the story into the conversation eliminates the possibility that the story will be followed by noticeable silence.

Failing to understand an appropriate, well structured story is a mark of conversational ineptitude on the part of the story recipients who can be reasonably expected to make "obvious" inferences and connections. However, because conversational stories are inherently no less "ambiguous" than literary texts, it is possible for there to be various legitimate interpretations of what the story was really "about." In the first place, stories can be thought to be "about" the main characters or objects involved and they can also plausibly be considered to be "about" the moral which can be inferred from the juxtaposition of the most important propositions. Since stories are complex utterances, a complex of responses may be appropriate. In the exit talk which follows "Eating on the New York Thruway," the first conversational story to be discussed, the first comment following the story itself is made by one of the recipients. Alan's question "Whadda they do to that?", neatly ties the poisoned coke to the incompetent restaurant staff who produced it, by asking for details of how the poisoning had come about. This response demonstrates both understanding of the point of the story and appreciation for the story, since Alan asked for more information about a story he clearly understood. The storytelling should be judged a successful effort.

3.3 "EATING ON THE NEW YORK THRUWAY"

"Eating on the New York Thruway" was told in the course of a dinner conversation in my home. Besides me, there were four other people present: Alan and Alice, a young married couple about to drive East from the Midwest, Carol, the teller of the story, and Bill, a common friend. Everyone spoke at least briefly during the telling. The situation which is described in the story took place during a trip which Carol and I had made from Michigan to New York sometime earlier. The comment which turned the talk to the New York Thruway followed a noticeable silence in the conversation and was topically unrelated to the talk which preceded it.

The analysis of "Eating on the New York Thruway" begins with a look at the entrance talk which led up to the telling of the story. (The numbers to the left of the text are reference numbers assigned to individual clauses. We shall refer to the clauses with these numbers in the following analysis.)

ENTRANCE TALK

1.	Alice:	I'm thinking of packing a lot of food and not eating on the road. There's something so depressing
	Bill:	Don't eat on the New York Thruway
5.	Livia:	Do NOT eat on the New York Thruway
	Carol:	Yeah, no don't it's
10.	Livia:	I think that's a good idea. I mean I'm not a picnicking person, generally. But
15.		God, the New York Thruway
	Alice:	Well, there're those
	Carol:	Even I, (laugh) what a mess
20.	Alice:	Well, it's the standard chain
	Livia:	No, it it's a million times worse
25.	Carol:	Yeah. You wouldn't believe it
	Alice:	I forget
30.	Carol:	I mean I mean Did I ever tell you the story about the water? I mean the coke?

When Carol announces that she has a story to tell, (Clause 30–31: *Did I ever tell you the story about the water, I mean the coke?*) she raises the expectation that she will tell a story involving water and coke and that would somehow make clear exactly why Carol (along with Bill and Livia) felt negatively about the food served in the restaurants on the New York Thruway. Because the story follows Carol's statement to Alice that . . . *[She]* . . . *wouldn't believe* . . . *[why the restaurants are a million times worse than the standard chain]* . ., the recipients were led to expect an "incredible" story, something more dramatic than merely having had indifferent food and poor service. In order to serve as an argument against the New York Thruway restaurants, *the story about the water, I mean the coke* needs to show those particular roadside places in a very bad light. And it does.

THE STORY

32. Carol: I went i . . . I always drink coke, right?
35. Livia: Right.
    Carol: So, Livia is thr . . . walking around with this gallon of spring water and I can't understand why she is walking around with
40.   this gallon of spring water. And she keeps talk . . . She keeps telling me these . . . vague making these vague remarks about the restaurants on the New York Thruway and at least we have
45.   this spring water and I don . . . I don't know
50.   what she's talking about. So we go to this restaurant and I order a coke and I ordered
55.   some sort of sandwich. Now, I don't think you ordered anything.
    Livia: I didn't order anything.
    Carol: Right
    Livia: I sat there making faces.
60. Carol: Well, one thing about this restaurant was that every person in it was retarded. (laughter)
65.   that's all. The people who worked there they were one after the other of the weirdest looking people I've ever (laughter) either they
70.   were retarded or they were let out for the day from the mental hospital. I . . . you know
    Livia: They didn't seem to be able to distinguish
75.   between washing the floor and making a hamburger. Both things were done in the same way. (laughter)
80. Carol: So, this coke appears. I was very thirsty. and I went like this (demonstrates) straw in took a sip of this coke and I started in screaming
85.   "I've been poisoned" and Livia very calmly handed me this spring water. I mean I have never in my life tasted anything so bad. (laughter)

Following the procedure for building an Adequate Paraphrase discussed in Chapter II results in these lists of Main Line Story Event, Story Durative-Descriptive, and Non Storyworld Clauses and corresponding lists of Mainline Story Event, Durative-Descriptive, and Non-Storyworld Propositions.

Main Line Story Event Clauses

32. I went i . .
50. we go to this restaurant
51. I order a coke
52. I ordered some kind of sandwich
79. this coke appears
81. I went like this (demonstrates)
82. [put the] straw in
83. took a sip of this coke
84. I started in screaming
86. and Livia very calmly hands me this spring water

Main Line Story Event Propositions

32/50. Carol and Livia went to the restaurant on the New York Thruway
    52. Carol ordered a coke
    52. Carol ordered a sandwich
    79. A coke appeared
81-82. Carol put the straw in the coke
    83. Carol took a sip of the coke
    84. <u>Carol started to scream</u> "I've been poisoned"
    86. Livia very calmly handed Carol the springwater.

Durative-Descriptive Clauses

33. I always drink coke.
37. Livia is thr
38. walking around with this gallon of spring water
40. and she keeps talk
41. She keeps telling me these
42. vague
43. making these vague remarks about the restaurants on the New York Thruway
44. and at least we have this spring water
45. and I don't
47. I don't know
48. what she's talking about
56. I didn't order anything
58. I sat there making faces
60. One thing about this restaurant was that
61. every person in it was retarded
64. the people who worked there
65. they were
67. one after the other of the weirdest looking people
68. I've ever
69. either they were retarded
70. or they were let out for the day from the mental hospital
73. They didn't seem to be able to distinguish between washing the floor and making a hamburger.
74. Both things were done in the same way.
80. I was very thirsty
85. "I've been poisoned."
88. I have never in my life tasted anything so bad.

Non-Storyworld Clauses

1. I'm thinking of packing a lot of food and not eating a lot on the road
2. There's something so depressing

3. Don't eat on the New York Thruway
4. Do NOT eat on the New York Thruway
5. Yeah
6. No
7. Don't
8. It's
9. I think
10. That's a good idea
11. I mean
12. I'm not a picnicking person generally
13. But
14. God
15. the New York Thruway
16. Well
17. There're those
18. Even I
19. What a mess
20. Well
21. It's the standard chain
22. No
23. It
24. It's a million times worse
25. Yeah
26. You wouldn't believe it
27. I forget
28. I mean
29. I mean
30. Did I ever tell you the story about the water?
31. I mean, the coke?
34. Right?
35. Right
46. you know
53. Now
54. I don't think (you ordered anything)
56. Well
62. that's all
63. I mean
66. I mean
72. You know
87. I mean

Non-Storyworld Propositions

    1a. Alice is thinking of packing a lot of food.
    1b. Alice is thinking of not eating a lot on the road. (i.e. not eating a lot in roadside restaurants)

2. Eating in roadside restaurants is depressing.

3. People should not eat at the restaurants on the New York Thruway.

9/10. It is a good idea not to eat at the restaurants on the New York Thruway.

12. Livia does not normally picnic.

15. The New York Thruway restaurants are too bad to eat in.

17. There are restaurants on the New York Thruway.

21. The restaurants on the New York Thruway are a standard chain.

22/24. The restaurants on the New York Thruway are a million times worse than the standard chain.

26. Alice would not believe how bad the restaurants on the New York Thruway are.

27. Alice forgot how bad the restaurants on the New York Thruway were.

54. Carol thinks that Livia did not order anything at the restaurant on the Thruway.

Durative-Descriptive Propositions

33. Carol always drinks coke.

(37. Livia was thr . . .)

38. Livia was walking around with a gallon of spring water.

39. Carol could not understand why Livia is walking around with a gallon of spring water.

37/40–43. Livia kept making vague remarks to Carol about the restaurants on the New York Thruway.

44. Livia kept telling Carol (in a vague way) that at least they had some spring water.

45/47/48. Carol did not understand what Livia was talking about.

55/56. Livia did not order anything.

58. Livia sat in the restaurant making faces.

60/61/64. Every person who worked in the restaurant was retarded.

64/65/67/68. The people who worked in the restaurant were the weirdest looking people Carol had ever seen.

64/69. The people who worked in the restaurant may have been retarded.

69/70. The people who worked in the restaurant may have been let out for the day from the mental hospital.

73/76. The people who worked in the restaurant were unable to distinguish between washing the floor and making a hamburger.

64/75–77. The people who worked in the restaurant washed the floors and made hamburgers in the same way.

80. Carol was very thirsty.

85. That she had been poisoned was screamed by Carol.

88. This coke was the worst thing Carol has ever tasted.

As described earlier, in order to put together an Adequate Paraphrase of the telling, the Main Line Story Event Propositions and Durative-Descriptive Propositions are examined individually and those propositions most highly evaluated by the devices operating in the text are singled out.

The analysis of the evaluation is summarized in the chart entitled "Evaluation in 'Eating on the New York Thruway'" which follows below:

CHART 3

Evaluation of Storyworld Propositions in "Eating on the New York Thruway"

Clause(s) Number	Clause Content (Proposition)	Story Event (E) or Durative Descriptive (D)	Contential Evaluators Which Evaluate the Proposition	Deictic Evaluators Which Evaluate the Proposition	Deictic Evaluation of Other Proposition by this Clause
32/50.	Carol and Livia went to a restaurant on the N.Y. Thruway	E			
33.	Carol always drinks coke	D		Appeal for confirmation outside storyworld	
37/40-3.	Livia kept making vague remarks about the restaurants on the N.Y. Thruway	D	Insistence on repetitive nature of comments. modification of remarks	Repetition of proposition.	
38.	Livia was walking around with a gallon of spring water	D		Repetition of proposition. in prop. 39.	(Spring water repeated)
39.	Carol could not understand why Livia is walking around with a gallon of spring water.	D	Negative encoding		Repeats prop. 38.
44.	Livia kept telling Carol (in a vague way) that at least they had some spring water	D	Insistence on repeated action.		(Spring water repeated)
45/7/8.	Carol did not understand what Livia is talking about	D	Negative encoding.	Repetition of "not understanding". External comment ("You know" cl. 46)	
51.	Carol ordered a coke	E			
52.	Carol ordered a sandwich	E	(Negative evaluation "some sort" of sandwich)		

(continued)

CHART 3 (*Continued*)

Clause(s) Number	Clause Content (Proposition)	Story Event (E) or Durative Descriptive (D)	Contential Evaluators Which Evaluate the Proposition	Deictic Evaluators Which Evaluate the Proposition	Deictic Evaluation of Other Proposition by this Clause
55/6.	Livia did not order anything	D	Negative encoding. Appeal for confirmation.	Repetition of proposition. Explicit removal from story world: "Now" cl. 53. Intrusion of narrator, cl. 54.	
58.	Livia sat in the restaurant making faces	D	"making faces"—unusual behavior.	Intrusion of story participant.	
60–1/64. 69	Every person who worked in the restaurant was "retarded" or may have been retarded	D	Hyperbole—"every person"	"One thing" points specifically to the "retarded" aspect. Explicit evaluator "That's all" cl. 62. Repetition (3x)	Repetition cl. 64, 69.
64–5/ 67– 8.	The people who worked in the restaurant were the weirdest people Carol had ever seen.	D	Hyperbole—"the weirdest people". Superlative. "one after another." Inverted syntax Exaggeration/speculation.	Specified further in cl. 60–1/64. 69/70. Intrusion of narrator cl. 63, 66, 68	
69/70.	The people who worked in the restaurant may have been let out for the day from the mental hospital.	D		Intrustion of narrator ("You know" cl. 72) 60–70 LOGICAL ARGUMENT	

73/76.	The people who worked in the restaurant were unable to distinguish between washing the floor and making a hamburger.	D	Mock logical argument. Convoluted syntax.	Specification of 60-1/64, 69.
79.	This coke appears	E	First event clause in 30 clauses. Short unattenuated clause. Agentless passive.	Intrusion of story participant. Specified cl. 77.
80.	Carol was very thirsty	D	Comparator.	Return to storyline, "So" clause 78.
81-2.	Carol put the straw in the coke.	E	Acted out. Abbreviated headless clause (cl. 82)	Clause 81. Deictic clause.
83.	Carol took a sip of the coke.	E	"this" coke. Collapses story-world and narrating world.	Proposition 84/5 evaluates the result of sipping the coke.
84.	Carol started to scream "I've been poisoned"	E	Screamed in narration	
85.		E	Only direct discourse	
86.	Livia calmly handed Carol the springwater.	E	Adverbially modified.	Points to cause of screaming—prop. 83.
88.	This coke was the worst thing Carol has ever tasted.	D	Hyperbole. Explicit evaluation. Intrusion of the narrator.	Points to the coke sipped in Prop. 83. Further specification.

The Durative-Descriptive Propositions which are most highly evaluated are:

> 39. Carol could not understand why Livia is walking around with a gallon of spring water.
>
> 64–65/67–69. The people who worked in the restaurant were the "weirdest" people Carol had evern seen (crazy and incompetent).

While the most heavily evaluated Story Event Proposition is:

> 83. Carol took a sip of the coke.

followed by:

> 86. Livia calmly handed Carol the spring water.

(Since 86. brings together Carol, Livia and the spring water to deal with the result of the 83—the poisoned coke—it should be included in the Paraphrase.)

Thus an Adequate Paraphrase of "Eating on the New York Thruway" could be:

> Carol was "poisoned" by sipping a coke prepared by weird incompetent people who worked at the restaurant on the New York Thruway. She was saved by Livia who had brought along (an otherwise mysterious) gallon of spring water.

Alan's comment immediately following the end of the story "Whadda they do to that?" began the exit talk and the absorption of the story into a general state of talk. This question which was delivered in tones of impressed bewilderment manages to encompass all of the vital elements of the core of the story: the coke, the incompetence of the staff in the restaurant, and the fact that they must have done something to make a coke so badly. During the remainder of the exit talk, there is a further description of the coke, a re-engagement of the storyworld with a corresponding increase in storyworld propositions, and finally a clear sign from Alice, the other recipient for whom the story was specifically told, that she had gotten the message. The incredible goings-on in the restaurant had apparently jarred her memory about the "horrible plazas or oases" on the highways and she and Alan would make their journey definitely via Ohio, thus making certain they would avoid the New York Thruway entirely.

EXIT TALK

> Alan: Whadda they do to that?
>
> 90. Livia: (laughing) You see, they also can't distinguish between making a coke and wringing out the mop.
>
> 95. Carol: Right . . . There is something I mean it was really something
>
> Alan: Yeah yeah . . . It's that bad

100.	Livia:	It comes out grey. Bright grey.
	Bill:	And very metallic
	Carol:	No. yeah it is metallic.
105.	Alice:	I can't bear . . . you know . . . you're driving and you're trying to make this mileage and you get out of the car and it's one of these horrible what do they
110.		call them? I forget.
	Alan:	Oases?
	Alice:	No. They have some
115.	Alan:	Plazas
	Alice:	PLAZAS
120.	Livia:	Mmmm hmmm. Oases are on . . . yeah on
	Carol:	On the way to Chicago.
	Alice:	It's horrible. I think we are going to
125.		We may drive through Ohio.

Both the incompetence of the restaurant staff and the exact nature of the poisoned coke are further specified before the storyworld is left definitively. The discussion moves to a more general condemnation of highway restaurants and then back to the topic of Alice and Alan's trip East. Thus, from the exit talk, the following propositions are added to the list of Durative-Descriptive Propositions:

New Durative-Descriptive Propositions

90–94. The people who work in the restaurant can't distinguish between making a coke and wringing out the mop.
100. The coke comes out grey.
101. The coke is bright grey.
102. The coke is very metallic.

The following clauses and propositions are added to the lists of Non-Storyworld Clauses and Propositions:

New Non-Storyworld Clauses

89. Whadda they do to that
90. You see
94. Right
95. There is something
96. I mean
98. Yeah Yeah
103. I can't bear
104. You know
105. You're driving
106. And you're trying to make this mileage

108. and it's one of those horrible
109. What do they call them?
110. I forget
111. Oases
112. No
113. They have some
114. Plazas?
115. PLAZAS
116. mmm hmmm
117. Oases are on the way to Chicago
118. It's horrible
122. I think
123. We are going to
124. we may drive through Ohio

New Non-Storyworld Propositions

100. The coke comes out grey.
101. The coke is bright grey.
102. The coke is very metallic.
103–115/121. Alice cannot bear trying to make (good) mileage and getting out of the car at a horrible plaza.
108–110. Alice has forgotten what the horrible plazas are called.
109–112. The horrible plazas are not called oases.
113. The horrible places which are not called oases have another name.
117–120. The oases are on the way to Chicago.
121–124. Alice thinks they are going to drive through Ohio.

Although it is possible to amend the Adequate Paraphrase to specify that the coke was grey, that seems hardly necessary. Nothing new is added to the Paraphrase in this exit talk. The recipients understood the point which was made and saw no need to dispute anything which had been said. The point of the story relates clearly back to the talk which was ongoing when the story was told. That talk continued on richer for the story but not re-focused or deflected by it. Having seen how this story functions as a "sequenced object" in the talk and how it is structured linguistically, what remains to be discussed is how this story is demonstrably designed to fit the personal and social situation obtaining at the moment of telling.

3.4 "RECIPIENT DESIGN" IN "EATING ON THE NEW YORK THRUWAY"

In order to understand exactly how the telling of "Eating on the New York Thruway" was influenced by the circumstances under which it was told, a number of different types of conditions must be taken into account. Important to consider are the exact nature of the relationships among the people present, their interest in each other, and their understanding of each others' habits and idiosyncrasies. The degree of involvement of the conversationalists in the incident itself is reflected in what is said (and by whom) while the use of "humor" and hyperbole is influenced by what the teller(s) felt would be acceptable to the others.

Carol's announcement of intention to tell about what had happened to her, while certainly a conventional gambit, was also a real question. Had the intended story recipients agreed that they *had* heard about the incident involving water and coke being alluded to, *Did I ever tell you the story about the water, I mean the coke* (Clause 30) might have led to the intended story recipients recapping the story, or Carol herself telling a very abbreviated version of it. She might merely have used the recipients' knowledge as a way of saying "See, that's what happens on the New York Thruway." As it turned out, no one indicated familiarity with the story and so Carol began her telling.

Almost immediately, she appealed to the recipients: (Clause 33–34) *I always drink coke, right?* and managed simultaneously to give Alan, Alice, and Bill some information about her (that she drinks coke), to make explicit to me that she knew my familiarity with her habits (since she appealed to me directly with her *Right?*), and to appear to include the others present in our more intimate circle. Had she used any one of a number of equally possible alternatives, she would have been unable to accomplish these three tasks so neatly. For example, had she left out the information about her coke drinking, her credentials as a cola-connoisseur might well have remained unknown to some of the others. Had she been a cola-innocent, she might well have tasted a perfectly acceptable sample of the beverage and still found it wretched. Therefore, to understand the story, it was important that everyone be aware of her expertise in this particular area.

She might have chosen to state this fact otherwise, of course. She might have stated that she "always drinks coke, as Livia knows." This formulation would have made clear that she and I were closer to one another than to some of the others. This would have run counter to our implicit agreement to act as if we were all equally close friends. Finally, had Carol merely stated that she always drinks coke and left it at that without asking me for confirmation, the closeness of our friendship would have been somewhat denied by placing me on exactly the same footing as the others vis à vis her special likes and dislikes. In fact, we were close friends and knew each other very well.

In addition, and much more central to this particular storytelling, is that I was a co-participant in the events recounted and a character in the story. This story, then, was partially about me and could not but function in some way as a comment on our friendship. To be coherent then, her behavior towards me in the telling had to match the comment she was making about me through the story. Otherwise, the story would function in the conversation as a message which was denied in the interaction as clearly as it was made in the telling.

By appealing to me immediately, Carol drew me into the telling. Having been invited to act as an "expert" and to say something, I was granted more access to the floor during the telling of the story than the others who were more purely "story recipients." In fact, this was most important in the present case because I was as much an expert on the common parts of the source experience as Carol was herself. Moreover, as became clear later on, I was more of an "expert" on the New York Thruway restaurants than Carol was before this misadventure.

All of the vague mumbling and mysterious walking around with the gallon of springwater which dominates the opening sections of the story might well have been played down in another telling. However, there are three circumstances which taken together explain the amount of prominence this mini-mystery is accorded. In the first place, Carol had announced that the story was to be about *the water* before she corrected herself, *I mean, the coke* (clauses 30–31). The subsequent story should make this slip seem reasonable by being *about water,* at least in part. Secondly, since I was present at the telling, that part of the story which most involved me was highlighted more than it might have been had I not been there.

The mystery of the spring water also underscores Carol's own ignorance of the true state of affairs at the Thruway restaurant before she had undergone the specific experience recalled in the story. Like Alice and Alan, she had thought it safe to eat in the restaurant and she had learned from her bad experience why *[Livia was] walking around with this gallon of spring water.* In other words, she was mystified and skeptical at the time by warnings of how dire the situation was, exactly as the recipients of her tale are at the moment of telling. What she learned from experience is, of course, what she hopes to impart to her friends. Therefore, Carol, the cokedrinker in the storyworld, is in the same relation to Livia, the water bearer, as Alan and Alice in the conversation bear to Carol, the narrator. The implicit message of the mystery is that they need not feel belittled by not knowing and by needing to be told.

As the story continues, Carol makes explicit that Livia did not order anything. Probably, had I not been there it would have been less necessary to make that clear. Perhaps it would not have been mentioned. Then, too, had she said something about it, she would most probably have merely stated that I did not order. She would not have exited from the storyworld and given her *theory* about what I had done ([Clauses 53–55] *Now, I don't think you ordered anything.*) Her doing so again reflects my status as co–participant and primary expert on my own behavior. Carol would probably omit Proposition 58, *Livia sat in the restaurant making faces* in another telling of the story, since it is not treated as an "omission" by either teller and Carol's response to it is marked as a *return* to the main story: *Well . . .* (Clause 59).

It is more difficult to make a strong case exactly *why* some material was included in this telling, but it seems reasonable to suppose that the remarks about the *weird looking people who were either retarded or let out for the day from a mental hospital* (Clauses 67–70) might well have been omitted altogether or phrased very differently had any of those present a (known) sensitivity either to retardation or mental illness.[1]

---

[1]When I have used this story in classes in The Netherlands, students always object to the "overstatement" of the narrator and recipients, in addition to feeling positively offended by the characterization of the restaurant personnel as crazy or mentally deficient. American "audiences", in classes and lectures have never *expressed* such difficulties with the story as told, although, of course many individuals might have reacted negatively and said nothing.

The use of hyperbole and exaggeration in this section of the story is also very clear. The story—recipients' feedback was important in order to establish that this sort of broad generalization was appreciated and understood.

Certainly the detailed description of the coke itself, as *bright grey* and *metallic* (Clauses 100–102) would be unlikely to turn up in another telling because this information was provided in response to prompting on the part of one of the recipients, Alan, who seemed to have been entirely convinced by the story. Although Alice never responded directly to the story, her very strong objection to the *oases or plazas* is clearly traceable to the story; before the story her characterization of the roadside restaurants as *the standard chain* was mild and almost positive.

Assembling and examining the lists of storyworld propositions reveals that many of them are related directly to the particular circumstances surrounding this specific telling. The Adequate Paraphrase which was built up is thus the paraphrase of this particular telling. On another occasion, prompted by other topics in a different embedding conversation and intended for recipients different from Alan and Alice, a telling using the incident of the poisoned coke as a basis might well amount to something other than an indictment of incompetence, and a celebration of fore-sightedness and rescue.

In Chapter Four, concerned with cultural presuppositions, each of the propositions in the Adequate Paraphrase of "Eating on the New York Thruway" will be considered again in order to determine the source of this story's impact. In the remainder of this chapter, however, the relationship between stories and conversation will be examined in greater detail. An example of a "diffuse story", a "story sequence," and a "negoti-ated story" are treated, in turn. Each of the texts under scrutiny are long and complex, involving intricate interactions among multiple speakers. Although "The Robbery," "Kate's Triumph," and "Fainting on the Subway" are very dense and rich in themselves, in order to limit the scope of the analyses somewhat, only those aspects of story structure which differ most from "The Baddest Girl in the Neigh-borhood" and "Eating on the New York Thruway" will be discussed at any length.

3.5 THE DIFFUSE STORY: "THE ROBBERY"

The "diffuse story" is characterized by blocks of story materials interleaved with blocks of conversation in which points of the story are discussed and amplified. The story begins with events which occurred earlier and moves to later events. The story may have several key events (although there is usually at least one) and there may be multiple core plots. What is striking about "The Robbery," which follows, is that it is at least as much a discussion of what did not happen as what did. The two women, Nancy and Susan, recount this story of a robbery at gunpoint, but evaluate most strongly that it is a story about how they might have been hurt.

"THE ROBBERY"

Bill: I heard second hand or whatever that you got robbed
Susan: Yeah

Bill: That's distressing. Was it near your house?

Susan: Yeah. We parked down at the hill you know . . . we were walking home. It was late at night and then this strange car pulled up and we thought "oh" it sounded a bit odd . . . and then this guy ran around and around to the back of it and he held this gun and said "Gimme your purse" and I said I didn't have one and I just gave him my wallet fast and he said to Nancy, he thought she was a guy, and "give me your wallet too." She said, "I don't have one" and he started feeling her, you know, and he had an actual gun (unintelligible)

Bill: You were what? You were walking up . . .

Nancy: It was loaded, too

Susan: Yeah

Nancy: It was loaded. I mean, I never doubted that it wasn't

Susan: You know, it was real scary cause you know at a whim he could have shot at us

Bill: Right

Susan: and you they were black and we were white and we thought any . . . you know

Nancy: So all I could think is "God is he going to take out everything on us?" It wouldn't have surprised me at all.

Susan: It was really scary

Nancy: Plus I keep saying, I said three or four times, "I don't have a wallet" but he couldn't seem to hear me. I guess because he was excited, you know, and I was getting . . . "Oh, my God is he going to shoot me because I don't have a wallet?"

Livia: (laugh) Oh, God

Nancy: You know, frustration you know . . . So . . . but he was actually thinking about, the one with the gun is not . . . he didn't . . . at first of course I was terrified seeing this person I didn't even know coming at me with a gun like out of a movie or something

Susan: It was really like a movie

2

Nancy: But the guy who was driving was the one that was really frightening

Livia: Uh, huh

Nancy: I mean he sounded like a maniac. I could not, I could

Susan: He was giving orders to the other guy

Nancy: not . . . But she didn't even hear him. You see she picked . . . she noticed all these visual things which I didn't notice. I really didn't notice

Susan: I didn't hear that guy in the car talking. Right?

Nancy: But he was shouting out things the whole time and I couldn't understand a word

Bill: He stayed in the car or whatever and

Susan: Yeah, he was in the driver's seat

Nancy: He was driving the car and and

Nancy: His voice was so filled with hate . . . I never

Susan: It was really something cause see also a lot of cars have trouble on that hill and sort of naturally slow down

Nancy: and, you know, I could not understand a word he said because it sounded like he had his mouth full of spit or something. I don't know. All I know, it was something ugly coming out. And that guy could hear him cause he was saying things like "Hey, the dude don't have a wallet" or something like that, that was me, boy, and then he yelled something back you know and he left and he yelled something before he left . . . and it was weird. He's the one who frightened me and the thing is he'll probably get off because nobody could identify him because he was in the car

Livia: Uh, huh

Nancy: Even though when they brought the first witness up—they'd just robbed another woman a few minutes earlier

Livia: Uh, huh

Nancy: He was standing by the cops with that guy and when he brought the woman up he said "That's the bitch" (laugh) and they got this . . . and also he said "I didn't do anything I was only driving the car." and I said "Isn't that enough to get him?" "You know, cause," I said. "He's the one who really worries me." I guess I said it about twenty times.

Susan: The other one was only sixteen, too. He was eighteen

Nancy: And they said "No, he'll get off on technicalities or something cause nobody can actually witness him." Of course, we never saw him.

Susan: And they both had a record of robberies and stuff like that with guns and everything but see, once you turn eighteen everything's dismissed. Did you know that?

Bill: You mean all the stuff that you did before

Susan: What?

Bill: All the stuff you did before . . . juvenile and so on

Susan: Yeah

Nancy: Right. Even though even though it was armed robbery—isn't that bizarre? I mean, I would personally rather be robbed by someone, say 25 or 30

Nancy: Than 16

Bill: without a gun

Nancy: Because I think they'd be a little more stable, you know, in general. It may not be true. They might just not . . . They might be even crazier.

Susan: It's crazy when your life is at the mercy of some maniac

3

Nancy: The police were all nice, you know. I'm happy to say

Susan: That was sort of like a movie itself, you know. We ca . . . we called the cops immediately and they came and they had already had the guys and so they took us in his car to where we had to identify them, you see

Livia: Uh, huh

Susan: Cause now they take the victims to the place, to them

Livia: Uh, huh

Susan: Instead of the opposite

Bill: How did they, uh

Susan: So they cruised up and down those hills and they found them and

Livia: Uh, huh

Susan: I said "Yes, that's him," but see we both thought the car they were driving was different. It was hard to see, you know

Nancy: But she said right away she told me it was a

Susan: Lincoln

Nancy: cream colored Lincoln. I had no idea what it was

Livia: Was it?

Susan: Yes (laugh)

Nancy: And that's how they caught them on the basis of

Susan: But I thought it was an older Lincoln you know because I know the backs of them, sort of

Nancy: And it had horrible broken muffler sound, you know

Susan: I actually know quite a lot

Bill: Oh

Nancy: Well

Bill: Well, so they were still driving around the neighborhood or something?

Nancy: Yeah. They were just a few blocks away

Susan: The cops had caught them by the time they came to our house which was about ten minutes which was amazing.

Nancy: Well, see, they were going on the basis of that other woman who said she said it was a long white car, white, you know

Susan: Dirty white

Nancy: Right. And they they had already stopped them and then they got our call

Livia: Uh, huh

Nancy: And so when they came they said "Come identify them. We've caught them." It was ridiculous. It was about five or ten minutes after

Bill: Weird. God.

Nancy: Well, it was just a few blocks from our house

Livia: Did you get your money back?

Nancy: Not yet

Livia: Oh, because it's evidence.

Nancy: And if they're not guilty we don't get it back and you know there're all these things this cop explained to us

Bill: Oh, you mean, you mean, if they, that is, if they, yeah, yeah, you mean if they aren't found guilty then then

Nancy: Right, with all this evidence. I mean, a few minutes later, but it's still . . . so, you know

Susan: You see, I tended to identify him basically on his clothes. He was wearing sort of this, uh, this jersey type . . . what do you call that material? Knit

Nancy: No, I don't think it was jersey, wasn't it just a sweater?

Susan: Yeah. It was a knit but it came long and I said even to her "It's green" and it was green

Nancy: Yes, she did. I said

Susan: she said

Nancy: I said "I don't know. Maybe he was wearing a leather jacket." I had no idea (laughter) I didn't notice anything

Bill: Well with one auditory person and one visual person you ought to be able to get a pretty good description there

Nancy: Well, my eyes were focused on the gun cause it was about a foot from my head.

Susan: He was holding it like a cop, you know, like that with both his hands.

Bill: Oh Jesus

Livia: Gooood

Nancy: If it ever happens to you, that cop says that's a very common reaction, you know, he said after you've been trained you can take your eyes off the gun cause you know it's there and you don't have to keep staring at it.

Livia: (laugh)

Nancy: And it's true . . . but I didn't . . . you, I was

Bill: Yeah, I wouldn't . . .

Nancy: Well, see, if I

Susan: I'm glad they didn't make one of us or both go with them or something, you know, with the gun . . .

Nancy: Right. Or just shoot us because, you know, for kicks or something. That's the the . . . It was the kind of thing that . . . It's terrible to be at the mercy of such people, you know

Susan: It makes you want to get a bullet-proof vest or something (laughter)

Susan: Has anything like that ever happened to you? Have you ever had your purse snatched?

The story has three main sections narrated more or less in the order one would expect had the story been told as one continuous unit: the robbery, the encounter with the driver, and finally, the incident with the police. (In the text, these sections are marked off from one another by spacing and numbering.) Section 1 details the actual action of being robbed. Discussion is concerned with the gun and the fact that the narrators were not murdered by their assailants though they might have been. Section 2 discusses the driver of the car and is an embedded story, or vignette, which evaluates the driver's behavior and raises the possibility that the robbers might not be prosecuted. Section 3 involves the interaction with the police themselves and Susan's skill in noticing visual details. The storytelling ends with a re-evaluation of the danger of the situation and the fact that Nancy and Susan were not killed.

The text is striking in that it is told by two narrators who talk back and forth to one another, amplifying, correcting, disagreeing, and resolving their differences in a continuous exchange. Therefore, the interaction has the "feel" of a conversation. In fact, however, the story recipients were, in the main, very passive and limited their remarks to an occasional *uh huh* or a short question or request for information (B: *He stayed in the car or whatever and*). Bill also makes some short remarks which are extended signals that he understood what went on. These comments serve similar functions to *uh huh* or *right*; they reassure the speaker that the message is getting through and that it is all right to continue (B: *Oh, you mean, you mean . . . if they, that is, if they . . . yeah . . . yeah . . . You mean if they aren't found guilty then then. . . .*).

Let us look at some examples of these storytellers' interaction. Amplification of one another's point pervades this text. For example:

Nancy: Well . . . see . . . they were going on the basis of that other woman said she
said it was a long white car you know
Susan: Dirty white.

Another example of amplification occurs when Susan reinforces Nancy's point:

Nancy: not . . . But she didn't even hear him. You see she picked . . . She noticed all
these visual things which I didn't notice. I really didn't notice.
Susan: I didn't hear that guy in the car talking, right?

The speakers also ask each other for support on details and reach for accord on what went on:

Susan: You see. I tended to identify him basically on his clothes. He was wearing this,
uh, jersey type . . . what do you call that material? Knit.
Nancy: No. I don't think it was a jersey, wasn't it just a sweater?
Susan: Yeah. It was knit but it came long and I said even to her "It's green" and it was
green.

Only once in the storytelling does a speaker explicitly involve the audience in the storytelling, asking directly if they had known about the situation with juveniles and the law before hearing her explanation:

Susan: And they both had a record of robberies and stuff like that with guns and
everything but see, once you turn eighteen everything's dismissed. Did you
know that?
Bill: You mean all the stuff that you did before
Susan: What?
Bill: All the stuff you did before . . . juvenile and so on
Susan: Yeah

However, the story continues to dominate the conversation. Rather than proceeding into a possible discussion of juvenile law, one speaker, Nancy, indicates that this problem acts to evaluate their story:

Nancy: Right. Even though even though it was armed robbery—isn't that bizarre? I
mean, I would personally rather be robbed by someone, say, 25 or 30.

This comment effectively narrows the possible topics of talk back to the original story by re-entering the storyworld, although subsequent talk makes it clear that this was a possible point of story closure:

Bill: than 16
Nancy: without a gun
Nancy: Because I think they'd be a little more stable, you know, in general. It may not
            be true. They might just not . . . They might be even crazier.
Susan: It's crazy when your life is at the mercy of some maniac.
Livia: Uh, huh

Susan's final comment works well for an evaluating remark on the entire story so far. After the pause, during which no story recipients indicate any response to the story or attempt to re-enter normal talk, the story resumes with a general, introductory remark about the police. This acts as an evaluative abstract for the next part of the story (Section 3). (See Sacks and Schegloff 1974 for a discussion of similar phenomena in conversation.)

Nancy: The police were all nice, you know. I'm happy to say.

The rest of Section 3 consists of a short narrative detailing their actual dealing with the police:

Susan: That was sort of like a movie itself, you know. We ca . . . we called the cops
            immediately and they came and they already had the guys and so they took us
            in his car to where we had to identify them, you see

There follows a short conversational interlude in which the search for the assailants is explained:

Livia: Uh, huh
Susan: Cause now they take the victims to the place, to them
Livia: Uh, huh
Susan: Instead of the opposite
Bill: How did they, uh
Susan: So they cruised up and down those hills and they found them, and
Livia: Uh, huh

This is followed by a relatively weakly evaluated actual identification of the men and a lively discussion of the car:

Susan: I said "Yes, that's him." But we both thought the car they were driving was
            different. It was hard to see . . . you know
Nancy: But she said right away she told me it was a
Susan: Lincoln
Nancy: cream colored Lincoln. I had no idea what it was
Livia: Was it?
Susan: Yes (laugh)
Nancy: And that's how they caught them on the basis of

Susan: But I thought it was an older Lincoln you know because I know the backs of
        them, sort of
Nancy: And it had . . . horrible broken muffler sound, you know
Susan: I actually know quite a lot
Bill: Oh
Nancy: Well

Interestingly, the overlapped portion of this section is the only one of three overlaps in the story in which Susan and Nancy were truly talking about different topics. Nancy is reaffirming the importance of her auditory knowledge (N: *And it had . . . horrible muffler sound, you know*) while Susan is reaffirming her visual knowledge (S: *I actually know quite a lot*) which refers to and generalizes her earlier claims to specialized information about the backs of Lincolns. This knowledge of cars and color identification of them, leads to a discussion of how the cops knew who the assailants were—they had been identified previously. Discussion culminates in a re-entry into the story, and a re-evaluation of the cops already having the guys from the earlier narrative segment:

Nancy: And so when they came they said "Come identify them. We've caught them."
        It was ridiculous. It was about five or ten minutes after.

The identification becomes increasingly more important as the conversation unfolds. Both Nancy and Susan concentrate on their own roles in the identification process:

Susan: You see, I tended to identify him basically on his clothes. He was wearing sort
        of this, uh, this jersey type . . . what do you call that material? knit.
Nancy: No, I don't think it was jersey, wasn't it just a sweater?
Susan: Yeah. It was a knit but it came long and I said even to her "It's green" and it
        was green
Nancy: Yes, she did. I said
Susan: She said
Nancy: I said, "I don't know. Maybe he was wearing a leather jacket." I had no idea
        (laughter) I didn't notice anything

Because Livia had asked a question somewhat earlier (L: *Did you get your money back?*), Susan and Nancy must interrupt their exposition of the story and act as proper conversational participants, answering the request for clarification. Nancy, who had been dwelling on the proximity of the assailants to their house before the question (N: *Well, it was just a few blocks from our house*), returns to that point after the question has been dealt with and both interlocutors satisfied with the answer (signalled by L's *Oh, because it's evidence*) and comment:

Bill: Oh, you mean, you mean, if they, that is, if they, yeah, yeah . . . you mean if
        they aren't found guilty then then
Nancy: Right, with all this evidence, I mean, a few minutes later, but it's still . . . so,
        you know

Nancy's comment (N: *Right with all this evidence*), adds no new information about the evidence or the judicial process, and then re-introduces the subject of the amount of time which had passed between the police being called and the thieves being arrested.

Bill's response to these remarks about the differences in abilities between Susan and Nancy accepts both of them and leads into the final wrap-up of the story:

Bill: Well with one auditory person and one visual person you ought to be able to get a pretty good description there

Nancy denies her lack of visual acuity (which she had worked rather hard to build up) and explains that she could not see because:

Nancy: Well, my eyes were focused on the gun cause it was about a foot from my head

This comment begins a conversation which returns the focus of attention to the gun, already heavily evaluated in the story's beginning:

Susan: He was holding it like a cop, you know, like that with both his hands (unintelligible)
Bill: Oh, Jesus
Livia: Gooood
Nancy: If it ever happens to you, that cop says that's a very common reaction, you know, he said after you've been trained you can take your eyes off the gun cause you know it's there and you don't have to keep staring at it.
Livia: (laugh)
Nancy: And it's true . . . but I didn't . . . you know, I was
Bill: Yeah, I wouldn't . . .
Nancy: Well, see if I

The story ends with a re-evaluation of the entire story in an extended coda detailing once again what did not occur:

Susan: I'm glad they didn't make one of us or both go with them or something, you know, with the gun . . .
Nancy: Right. Or just shoot us, because, you know, for kicks or something. That's the the . . . It was the kind of thing that . . . It's terrible to be at the mercy of such people, you know

This is followed by a short epigrammatic comment and then Susan turns to the patient recipients and asks them to tell their own stories:

Susan: It makes you want to get a bullet proof vest or something (laughter)
Susan: Has anything like that ever happened to you? Have you ever had your purse snatched?

One particularly important feature of the diffuse story is that the evaluation of crucial material is accomplished largely through the turntaking system of the conversation.

In the other stories discussed so far, evaluation is accomplished mainly through lexical and sentence level devices with some additional discourse devices such as delaying the course of the action. Much evaluation in diffuse stories is carried out by the storytellers who act as conversational partners, taking up various themes in the story as topics of conversation. Thus while the actual narration of the Main Line Story Events in this telling was a somewhat bald presentation of what happened, in the discussion which followed in Section 3, both the identification of the assailants first mentioned as an event (Susan said, "Yes that's him.") and the car which the assailants were driving were evaluated by extensive conversational exchange.

The diffuse story provides a strategy for telling a very long story with significant emotional impact but few events. The tellers engage in pseudo-conversation through which all of the short, purely narrative sections are expanded and thoroughly contextualized and explored. This medium offers opportunity and a flexibility for eliciting and being responsive to the reactions of the recipients. Since the storytellers are quite actively conversing as well as storytelling, they are relieved of the responsibility for keeping the action going. In addition they need not determine exactly which potentially interesting material ought to be conventionally structured and evaluated at the expense of other material. (See 4.6 below for discussion of cultural presuppositions in this story based on an Adequate Paraphrase of the most highly evaluated propositions.)

3.6 THE STORY SEQUENCE: "KATE'S TRIUMPH"

The "story sequence", "Kate's Triumph," discussed below differs from "The Robbery" in three important respects. First, there is more than one story told, and the stories are told as more or less self-contained units, some of which are embedded within others. Second, there is one primary narrator for each story, although more than one storyteller is involved in telling stories at various points in the sequence. The secondary storytellers, who were also involved in the circumstances being discussed and knew enough to have told the same—or similar—story, act more or less as story recipients while the story is being told. Though the primary storyteller is prompted by secondary storytellers, there is no real competition for the floor and the talking remained clearly "storytelling" and not a pseudo-conversation. Third, the evaluation in the stories which makes up the sequences is, for the most part, internal to the storyworld clauses.

"Kate's Triumph" is an example of a story sequence: a long story telling interaction which is difficult to break down absolutely into its constituent parts. The storyworld propositions may arguably be divided into a group of stories interacting either as a simple chain of one story after another; as a hierarchically embedding structure of major stories which embed minor ones within them as vignettes; or as one very large story, hierarchically embedding several major stories which appear independent as they are being told but which link up into one grand unit at the end of the sequence.

"THE ORDEAL"

Tom: Right. We'd all gone through this ordeal with the stitching and the unstitching and the bleeding and uh . . . you know Kate having . . . essentially . . . what could have been considered surgery done without anything but a local anaesthetic. (B: hm) . . . uh . . . which meant that she was awake and crying out whenever something hurt especially all the pressure (L: mmm) and uh . . . that was not so bad for Kennedy but this Meyers guy, the bowel man (laughter) was really freaked out by it. He's coming up into obstetrics (K: Kennedy was upset, too) delivery room "What's going on here? What are you doing? (laughter)

Livia: Oh, no Kate. "What baby?"

Tom: "What is this?" Well, you know we went through two hours of that . . . and then . . . you know . . . Kate was all ready to see the . . . to see Adam you know she was all pale (laughter) and in need of blood and she's asking a million questions (laughter) UH . . . let's see . . . "Will I be able to get a private room?" (K: laugh) "Can I have the baby in the room tomorrow?" (laughter) "Is it alright even if I'm on the I–V?" Uh "If I can't eat, when can I drink?" "When you say I can't have many liquids how much liquids can I have?" (laughter) "Will I be able to start nursing tomorrow?" and just on and on and on you know she . . . you know you know they're . . . meanwhile they're attaching the I–V putting the water in you know and (laughter) and uh . . . and Kennedy was answering all these questions being very maternal (laughter) and uh . . . finally she said to Kate "Do you have any questions?" (loud general laughter) (very soft distinctive voice) and I guess then Kate asked her "Well, you know, well, what really happened? you know . . . and . . . uh . . . and she said . . . "I'll give it to you straight" uh . . . "You didn't have an enema and there was shit in your ass" (laughter) "and when the baby came out it tore your ass" (laughter)

Tom: "Are you happy now? Are you satisfied?" (laughter)

Kate: "And the doctor's afraid you're going to get infected."

Tom: Oh . . . yeah . . . he's afraid there's going to be an infection and that's why you can't eat and we don't want you to shit for a few days . . . and . . . uh . . . Kate is lying back there her lips absolutely white . . . her arms are . . . you know . . . she's half dead and she points up and she says to Kennedy (K: laugh) "That's what I like about you" (laughter) "You tell everything straight." (general laughter)

Kate: Tom, too. It was great

Tom: Yeah . . . you were terrific

"INTERLUDE"

Kate: My father came to see me . . . I don't know Adam was it was the second day after Adam was born or something . . . and he's riding in the elevator and saying to us . . . and people talking about Brown Brown (laughter) "What is this?" (laugh)

"THE WALK"

Tom: You know . . . you know . . . they moved Kate from a semi-private to a private
room after . . . after she had slept that night . . . and uh . . . the semi-private
was in one end of the w . . . way over in on one end of the hospital and the
private was way over on the other . . . and . . . uh . . . she was terrified that
sitting on the stitches would hurt . . . so she walked . . . you know from one end
to the other (laughter) this became a story (K: laugh). I mean . . . then nurse's
aides would come in and . . . they would say "she walked with her I–V all the
way from one end of this hospital" (laughter)

Bill: dragging the I–V behind her

Kate: Well, they didn't know that basically I was terrified. I mean this friend of mine
had talked to me about . . . uh . . . cousins of hers that wouldn't sit down for
two weeks after they had the baby I said (alteration of voice as if mimicking
speech) "Oh God, that must hurt like hell" (sotto voice). I wasn't going to do it.
Here I'd been through labor which . . . you . . . um . . . is an inCREDible
expenditure of energy. You know . . . and after this I'm hooked up to this I–
V . . . and . . . it was blazing hot and I was sweating . . . and I was (laugh)
starving

Tom: You were dehydrated

"HOSPITAL HIERARCHY"

Kate: I was dehydrated . . . and . . . uh . . . the . . . uh . . . there's this descending
hierarchy in the hospital . . . um . . . you know there's your doctor . . . and then
there are the residents who check you when your doctor's not around.

Tom: FIRST there's the surgeon (K: Mm, right, yeah) Meyers was the surgeon

Kate: Oh yeah, right Kennedy really deferred to Meyers which was a very interesting
thing to see. Then there are the delivery room nurses that are really
terrific . . . then there are the nursery nurses who seem to like holding
babies . . . (laughter) then there are nurses' aides . . . (T: right) . . . who come
into your room and they don't know anything . . . it's like when I first checked
into the hospital, there was a nurses' aide . . . it was her first day on duty and
you know I wasn't really in labor . . . and . . . um . . . you know . . . I walk into
this hospital room and "I'm new here and I don't know what I'm supposed to
do." (laughter) and you know basically they were all like that and . . . I
mean . . . you know.

Tom: They go around and they take temperatures and strip the beds (yeah)

Kate: I mean . . . they couldn't give you an aspirin. It's like you could tell them you
want an aspirin and someone higher up will bring you an aspirin (mm) . . . it's
that sort of thing . . . Um . . . and then the lowest of the low . . . are the
cafeteria PEOple . . . (T: right) and they're incredibly young and dumb and so
on . . . that first morning or the second morning they brought me a breakfast
and I was hysterical because here was this smell of food (L: Oh, God) and I went
out of my mind and I just screamed I said "Take that out! That's not for me!"
You know and basically I just wanted to eat it (laugh) and disobey . . . you know

> but . . . they said "It has your name on it. It's yours." And I shook this I–V and
> I said "I'm on an I–V, I can't eat. Take it out of here!" (laughter) at which point
> the bowel man appears (laughter) magically and he said "I see your lungs are all
> right!" (long period of general laughter)

We will work sequentially through the text, beginning with "The Ordeal" and
working through until the end concentrating on information about story sequences in
conversations not covered previously. In this discussion the third story, "Hospital
Hierarchy," will receive the bulk of attention much as Section 3 did in the analysis of
"The Robbery."

"Hospital hierarchy" ties the entire sequence together into one super-story. Each
seemingly independent story acquires the status of a sub-unit of the super-story and
works in concert with other sub-units to create a coherent story-structure.

In his monologue Tom describes Kate's difficulty during the delivery up to the
doctor's final answer to Kate's question. At this point Kate breaks in, evaluates the
doctor's attitude in a pseudo-quote and then continues with an actual piece of direct
discourse. Tom continues the story which ends with Kate's remark to the doctor.
This remark re-evaluates the doctor's comment and clarifies that the evaluated material is not the scatalogical information, but rather the straightforward presentation of
it.

Tom: and uh . . . finally she said to Kate "Do you have any more questions?"; (loud
       general laughter) (very soft distinctive voice) and I guess then Kate asked her
       "Well, you know, well, what really happened?" you
       know . . . and . . . uh . . . and she said . . . "I'll give it to you straight"
       uh . . . "You didn't have an enema and there was shit in your ass" (laughter)
       "and when the baby came out it tore your ass" (Laughter)
Tom: "Are you happy now? Are you satisfied?" (laughter)
Kate: "And the doctor's afraid you're going to get infected."
Tom: Oh . . . yeah . . . "he's afraid there's going to be an infection and that's why you
       can't eat and we don't want you to shit for a few days" . . . and . . . uh . . . Kate
       is lying back there her lips absolutely white . . . her arms are . . . you
       know . . . she's half dead and she points up and she says to Kennedy (K: laugh)
       "That's what I like about you." (laughter) "You tell everything straight." (general
       laughter)

Following the general laughter which greeted the story and signalled its acceptance
by the other people present, Kate ambiguously validates both the entire childbirth
experience and the doctor's treatment of her:

Kate: Tom, too. It was great.

Tom responds to Kate by pointing to Kate's behavior during the birth process and
once again emphasizes that the story is about Kate's spirit and endurance:

Tom: Yeah . . . you were terrific

Kate then begins what appears to be a story, but which actually is an evaluative remark about her entire hospital stay. Not only Tom and Kate thought that their experience was unique and therefore storyworthy but the entire hospital was talking about it:

Kate: My father came to see me . . . I don't know Adam was it was the second day after Adam was born or something . . . and he's riding in the elevator and saying to us . . . and people talking about Brown Brown (laughter) "What is this?" (laugh)

Tom then begins the second major story, "The Walk," which in his version has the same point as his explicit external evaluation of "The Ordeal": Kate was terrific. Kate, however, takes over the story after Tom had completed narrating the events and presents a short vignette explaining *why* she walked. This explanation re-establishes her human fallibility and creates a new type of solidarity with the story recipients who otherwise might have felt themselves permanently one-upped by such a display of courage. Acting as an intermediary between teller and audience is one of the functions of a secondary storyteller who can spur the primary teller on to tell a more interesting story, or re-evaluate material in the story to make it more credible or otherwise acceptable to the audience (Sacks, 1971).

Kate then tells the third story, "Hospital Hierarchy," which is structured in an exceedingly interesting manner. The story is not only temporally structured as most American stories are, but also mirrors the descending hospital hierarchy which it describes. At each step down the hierarchy there is commentary on the type of person who is at that level. The doctors and surgeon are mentioned only as being on the top. The delivery room nurses, one step down the ladder, are given a bit more color (K: . . . *Then there are the deliveryroom nurses that are really terrific.*) The nursery nurses, another step down, are simply dismissed (K: [*they*] . . . *seem to like holding babies*) while the nurses' aides merit an entire vignette detailing their incompetence and general uselessness. The action of the story involves an interaction between Kate and the cafeteria workers:

Kate: Um . . . and then the lowest of the low . . . are the cafeteria PEOple . . . (T: right) and they're incredibly young and dumb and so on . . . that first morning or the second morning they brought me a breakfast and I was hysterical because here was this smell of food (L: Oh, God) and I went out of my mind and I just screamed I said "Take that out! That's not for me!" You know and basically I just wanted to eat it (laugh) and disobey . . . you know but . . . they said "It has your name on it. It's yours." And I shook this I–V and I said "I'm on an I–V, I can't eat. Take it out of here!" (laughter) at which point the bowel man appears (laughter) magically and he said "I see your lungs are all right!" (long period of general laughter)

The unexpected appearance of the bowel man, from the top of the hierarchy and from the very first story, into an interchange between Kate and the cafeteria worker from the bottom of the hierarchy creates a magic moment in the storytelling. The hierarchy collapses as both ends of the scale come together. In telling her story, Kate uses the deictic *this* to describe her I–V and shakes her arm as if shaking the I–V and shouts in the conversational setting as she shouts in the story. This acts to collapse the time frames of the storytelling and the story into one powerful moment which simultaneously evaluates her strength as a person (one main point of the story) and the intensity of the experience (the other point). The doctor's final remark which finishes the story (K: . . . *he said "I see your lungs are all right"*) adds even more to the collapse of all time frames since two of Kate's more immediately striking attributes are her strong speaking voice and exceptional verbal forthrightness. These attributes were present in the storytelling context, in the third story, and also in the first story which could also have been summed up by someone saying "I see your lungs are all right."

This collapse of all time frames and important characterological material into one instant in the third story leads to the argument that one could consider the whole of "Kate's Triumph" to be one story which culminates in the key evaluative remark in the core plot of the third story. However, each of the sub-stories composing the super–story is distinct. Each story unit could easily stand alone and indeed appears to do so as we proceed through the text. (The vignettes do not really stand alone as told, although they contain enough information from which to fashion a story.) The short "Interlude" in which Kate describes her father riding up in the elevator and overhearing everyone talking about her is not really a story, because it has no point beyond its evaluative effect on the other stories. This question of what can be taken to be the point of a story and what kinds of material provide enough support for the claim being made for the story by the speaker's evaluation of it is discussed below in connection with negotiating the point of a story.

3.7 THE NEGOTIATED STORY: "FAINTING ON THE SUBWAY"

Story texts, as we have seen, are often complex and bewildering. We may well have a difficult time understanding the boundaries between the conversation and the story, and, in the case of the diffuse story, we may be quite justified in questioning the meaningfulness of such a division into story and nonstory. In interactively constructed discourse, such as conversational storytelling, "meaning" is not an absolute characteristic of texts. In the course of an interaction, proposals for what is going on in the telling may be brought forward by the teller through internal evaluation and explicit commentary and may be disputed by the conversational recipients who may offer their own interpretations of what the telling should be taken to be about. In the remainder of this chapter, we will examine one story, "Fainting on the Subway," in some detail, in order to illustrate the notion of "negotiating the point" of a story.

"Fainting on the Subway" was elicited by Deborah Tannen from one of three or four women in answer to the question "Have you ever had any interesting experiences on the subway?" (It appears here with her permission.) The narration of events and descriptive information was interrupted several times by everyone present (including the storyteller) who asked questions, made comments, laughed, and made sounds of assent. The storyteller resumed speaking after each interruption and backtracked in her story, offering new information about the time of the incident, and made general comments dealing with those conditions of her life and in the world which she considered her story to be illustrating. Most people listening to or reading this text for the first time find it highly complex and confusing, with a great deal of extraneous material getting in the way of the story. Upon closer examination, it appears that what is going on can best be viewed as "negotiation" between narrator and audience about what is to be taken as the point of the story.

"Fainting on the Subway"

In order to characterize this text as a "negotiation," a model of what a "negotiation" involves is needed. Let us take the simplest possible model, and assume that there must be negotiators, something on the table to be negotiated about, proposals and counterproposals put forward, backed by supporting evidence, argumentation, or other manifestations of power, and finally, either resolution of the issue on the table or an impasse reached. All of these features are present in some form in the "Fainting on the Subway" text: the negotiators are the speaker and her audience, specifically those who question and challenge her. Her reputation in the group as both a good storyteller and competent member of society is at stake along with the point of the story she has told. The resolution comes with the speaker re-evaluating her story as illustrating a point all agree is both storyworthy and properly backed up by the story materials; then the discussion moves on to a new story.

In Chapter Four it is argued that the proposals and counterproposals put forward in a process of negotiating the point of a story are backed by culturally salient presuppositions held jointly by speaker and audience about what is right, wrong, normal, abnormal, a necessity of life, and so on.

"FAINTING ON THE SUBWAY"

A: I just had . . . two p . . . particular incidents that I remember . . . and one-
uh- . . . [I] neither one of them really had . . . any kinds of endings or anything,
that you know resolution, they just happened . . . um . . . ONE of them was-
uh- . . . back in . . . what 66? . . . 67 . . . when [?] I (?) FAINted on the
subway . . . It was very um . . . uh . . . FRIGHTening experience . . . I had
DON'T even remember FAINTing before in my life let alone on the
subway . . . And uh- . . . it was a h . . . very hot . . . August day . . . and I was
going into the city . . . from Queens? . . . A-nd . . . I was standing . . . in a very
crowded car . . . And I remember standing . . . I was standing up . . . and I
remember holding on to the . . . center pole . . . and . . . I remember (chuckle)

saying to myself . . . there is a person over there that's falling to the
ground . . . And that person was me . . . And I couldn't . . .

B: Oh, wow

A: . . . put together the fact . . . that . . . there was someone fainting and that
someone was me . . . And I just fell down . . . (clears throat) then all of a sudden
there was a lot of space, and . . . people . . . helped me up, and . . . someone sat
me down . . . A-nd then-uh- . . .

B: It wasn't rush hour

A: Yes it was . . .

B: Yeah?

A: That's . . . partly why I fainted . . .

B: Mm

A: Uh . . . I was under . . . tremendous . . . emotional pressures at the time, . . .

B: Mm

A: and personal . . . pressure . . . and . . . the crush . . . of the BODIES . . . and the
no [?] AIR in the CAR . . . and everything just kind of combined . . .

B: Mm

A: A-nd um- . . . it was incredibly HOT, . . . a-nd uh- . . . we waited . . . until the
next stop, (low pitch and amplitude -----------) which was just a few minutes
away . . . and then . . . someone took me off . . . the car, . . . and (sighs) he got a
policeman . . . and . . . he came over . . . and asked what was wrong, and he asked
me just two questions. Are you pregnant? . . . To which I said no. I mean
they . . . like he was told that I had fainted . . .

B: (chuckle)

A: A-nd uh, . . . uh he said . . . in a very embarrassed kind of way do you have your
period now . . .

B: (laugh)

A: And I said no . . . A-nd then he said OK and he sat me down, and they got an
ambulance . . . and the ambulance ca-me, and took me to . . . a nearby
hospital . . . A-nd u-m . . . I just stayed in the . . . emergency room . . . for . . . I
guess an hour . . . It was it was heat prostration . . . A lot of it . . .

B: Mm

A: Having eaten . . . having . . . having not had . . . not . . . EATen . . . for several
DA-YS . . .

B: uh

A: and . . . I was job hun [?] it was just . . . a whole mess . . . BUT . . . u-m
. . . AFTER THAT, . . . I could not . . . ride . . . on the subway . . . And to this
day I have trouble . . . riding on the subway . . . If I'm with someone I feel
OK. . . . If I'm alone, . . . IN rush hour . . . I c . . . I . . . c-ant. If . . . I'm very
very scared of . . . fainting again . . . Um . . . I don't know if you've ever

B: Um

A: experienced . . .

B: I haven't

A: . . . There is NO experience in the WORLD . . . like experiencing . . . rush
hour . . . in the subway . . . Uh- . .

B: Oh, rush hour. Not fainting

A: Yeah. The closest thing I can compare it to, and I never experienced

THAT . . . and it's probably a FRACtion of what THAT experience was, . . . but I think . . .

B: Mm

A: of the way the Jews . . . were herded

B: Mm

A: into the cattle cars . . . Tsk and that's . . . you know . . . maybe . . . maybe part of THAT . . . ties into that . . . kind of . . .

B: Yeah

A: thing . . . And I just panic . . . I mean . . . everything in me . . . freezes up, and I can't do it . . .

B: Mm

A: And it's just as dehumanizing . . .

B: But people were pretty nice, hm?

A: People . . . are . . . Always nice when there's a crisis like that . . . And . . . and the context was right . . . I was WHITE, . . I was a young woman . . . I was w-ell dressed, I was . . . obviously not . . . a pervert, or a deviate, . . . or a criminal . . .

B: (laugh)

A: HAD I BEEN . . . had I been . . . anything OTHER than that . . . I could've fallen . . . and they would've stepped OVER me . . . Or perhaps ON ME . . .

B: (laugh)

A: You know cause that's the way people in New York ARE.

C: Didn't you used to grab the strap . . . in the subway?

A: I was just saying . . . I . . . yeah. . . . But I was in . . . standing in the center of the car, holding onto the center POLE, . . . and I just slid down the pole. . . . A-nd uh- . . . it was funny because . . . in my HEAD . . . I said . . . my aWAREness was such . . . that . . . that I said to myself . . . gee wizz there's a PERson over there, falling DOWN. And that person was me.

B: It's weird . . . mm

A: Ok that was . . . that experience

The following list of proposals for what the story told by the speaker should be taken to be about will be developed at some length through the rest of this chapter. The reader may find it helpful to refer to this list as well as to the story itself while proceeding through the discussion.

Proposals for Meaning

1. Fainting on the subway is frightening.
   (Proposed by speaker through comments and internal evaluation of her story.)
2A. Personal problems in the past are important.
   (Proposed by speaker in response to B's comment indicating lack of proper response to the story.)
2B. Personal problems in the present are even more important.
   (Proposed by speaker at end of narrative portion of story.)
3. Rush hour is as terrible as living through Nazi concentration camp horrors.

(Proposed by speaker following recital of present-day difficulties resulting from the fainting episode.)

4A. People are nice.
   (Proposed by B—citing evidence of how strangers treated speaker as proof of people being "human" not "dehumanized.")

4B. People aren't *really* nice—they are bigots.
   (Proposed by speaker in answer to B claiming that the people B naively thought "nice" were not. They would not have been helpful to someone who was really strange or threatening to them.)

5. People are like that in New York.
   (Proposed by speaker, as something that could be a compromise position. Everyone knows New Yorkers are scarcely human at best.)

6. Speaker is an inept subway rider.
   (Proposed by C—since speaker fell, perhaps she did not know how to ride the subway properly.)

7. Fainting warps perception.
   (Initially speaker included this proposal as part of her description of fainting—but she put little stress on the point. At the end of the text she re-enters the narrative at the moment of fainting and evaluates her awareness of herself fainting as the interesting materials using internal evaluative devices.)

The speaker does not choose to highlight a part of her story which could have been emphasized. This missing proposal, that men are convinced that whatever happens to women happens because of their "biological functioning," will be known as *Men Are All Like That* and it will be discussed after the others. Discussing an event which is not evaluated, but might have been, can give some interesting insight into the process of evaluation and the choices narrators make about the treatment of their story materials.

3.7.1 NEGOTIATING THE POINT OF A STORY

The speaker begins her story with the comment that she remembered two particular incidents on the subway. She proposed that the point of her story will be that she fainted while on the subway and that this was a very frightening experience. Her opening remarks are highly evaluated:

A: I FAINTed on the subway . . . It was very um . . . uh FRIGHTening experience. I had DON'T ever remember FAINTing before in my whole life, let alone on the subway.

She uses heightened stress, repetition, and, most interestingly, a negative proposition, i.e. a statement of something which did not happen to impress upon her audience both the uniqueness of the event in her life and its frightening quality.

The amount of evaluation attached to the falling down itself clarifies that fainting is the key event in the story:

> A: I remember saying to myself . . . there is a person over there that's falling to the ground . . . And that person was me . . . And I couldn't put together the fact . . . that . . . that there was someone fainting and that someone was me . . . And I just fell down. (clears throat)

The amount of discussion before the act itself, the discussion of the altered awareness, the putting forward of a negative proposition (what she couldn't *put together*) and finally the simply stated event, *I just fell down,* act to spotlight the act of fainting. This is the first event in the narrative structure of the story; it is the first, unqualified remark the speaker has made. Thus it contrasts starkly with the surrounding, rather discursive, contextualizing material. However, nothing particularly frightening happens to her as she is fainting or after she faints.

When B comments *"It wasn't rush hour,"* the speaker knows that she had not really set the scene for her story or justified why this fainting spell had occurred. Realizing that she is losing her audience, she puts forward Proposal 2, *Personal problems,* and suggests that she fainted because she was having difficulties in her life at that time. Although she says that it was, in fact, rush hour, she goes on to volunteer personal information about the *tremendous emotional pressure* she was under at the time of the incident. There is no reason to believe that this whole issue of *pressure* would have been introduced, at least not at this time, without B's remark. The teller's *And then* which preceded B's question indicates that the speaker was about to go on with the narrative events and not pause for evaluative or descriptive details. By divulging the seemingly extraneous information that she was under pressure, the speaker assures the audience that this is no mere story about a fainting spell, but also sheds light on her emotional life. The idea of personal pressure is evaluated by repetition:

> A: I was under . . . tremendous . . . emotional pressure at the time . . . and personal . . . pressure

The use of the intensifier *tremendous* also acts to reinforce the importance of the statement. The speaker goes on to give several details of the conditions in the subway car, and the conditions in her life which *just sort of combined . . . (into) . . . a whole mess.* Before continuing with the narrative events, she says:

> A: the crush of the bodies . . . and the no . . . AIR in the CAR, . . . and everything just kind of combined. . . . a-nd um . . . it was incredibly HOT

After finishing with the narrative portion, she comments:

A: Having eaten . . . having . . . having not had . . . not EATen for several
     DAYS . . . and I was job hunting it was just a whole mess.

A great deal of repetition, hesitation, heightened stress, and the choice of *the crush of the bodies* as an encoding for *crowded,* combine to give a very vivid impression of exactly what *personal pressure* is involved.

The speaker demonstrates that this period was a very storyworthy one, because it differed so widely from the way things ought to be. She does not stop with detailing her problems in the past, however, but continues to tell how the effects of this time and this incident continue on into the present. A story with ramifications for the present moment is most certainly narratable:

A: And to this day I have trouble . . . riding on the subway. If I'm with someone I feel
     OK . . . If I'm alone, . . . IN rush hour, I c . . . I c-an't. If . . . I'm very very scared
     of . . . fainting again.

She uses few evaluative devices in this section, although the hesitation and self-correction are unusual and evaluatory in the sense that they almost act out the effects of being afraid and under the spell of that experience. Her increased stress on the *in* of *in rush hour* makes certain that no one will misunderstand and assume she fainted without cause. The double intensifier *very very,* which is common in many discourses, is only found in this one instance in this text, lending it increased weight. If past problems are interesting, present ones are that much more so.

By bringing the effects of this experience into the present, the speaker is bringing it closer to her audience-insisting that this is not merely a story about the past, but is, in fact, a story about the present and an explanation of why she is less than totally competent at carrying out the comings and goings of everyday life.

Unfortunately, the speaker did not stop with demonstrating how this story could account for important aspects of her present life, but insisted that, in fact, this story shows how rush hour in the subway is one of the worst and most unusual experiences in the world.

A: I don't know if you've ever . . . experienced . . .
B: I haven't
A: There is NO experience in the WORLD, . . . like experiencing rush hour . . . in
     the subway . . . uh . . .
B: Oh, rush hour. Not fainting.

Her own life, past and present, is interesting and storyworthy but since the elicitation question had to do with the *subways* not merely with personal events, she must somehow link her feelings of pressure, heat, and discomfort with some general fact about subways. B's interjection *Oh, rush hour. Not fainting.* seems to be a surprised reaction to the violation of the expectation that the speaker had set up when she followed *I don't know if you've ever experienced* with a discussion of rush hour instead of continuing with the preceding theme—*fear of fainting again.* (B may have been particularly surprised since she knows that the speaker knows B to be a New Yorker who presumably would have been on the subway, under all types of conditions.)

Proposal 3, *Rush hour is as terrible as living through Nazi concentration camp horrors,* is the most highly evaluated proposal, but it is not accepted by the audience:

A: Yeah, the closest thing I can compare it to, and I never experienced THAT . . . and it's probably a FRACtion of what THAT experience was, . . . but I think . . . of the way the Jews . . . were herded into the cattle cars . . . Tsk and that's . . . you know . . . maybe . . maybe part of that . . . ties into that . . . kind of thing. And I just panic . . . I mean . . . everything in me . . . freezes up, and I can't do it . . . And it's just as dehumanizing

All of the qualification acts to reinforce the comparison Speaker is making. *Tsk, I mean,* and *you know,* which are very common in the speech of many people, are found almost nowhere else in this text. The *you know* acts in concert with the unfinished question she asked B and creates an appeal to the audience. The speaker gives the impression that any good person must understand the implications (and thus the truth) of what she is saying by her strong insistence on *that,* together with her faith that the audience knows the full extent of the evils concealed in the stressed and repeated *that,* the referent of which is clearly the Nazi atrocities, summoned up with the rather formal, almost literary, *the way the Jews were herded into the cattle cars.* The triple *the* acts to impress the certainty of the belief the speaker has in her listeners knowing that the reference is to the Nazis, who epitomize everything that men ought not to be, and to life in the concentration camps, which epitomizes everything life should not be. This is an example of what might be called "evaluation by touchstone"—anything which is compared to the horror of Nazi Germany is highlighted by the strength of the reaction to the concentration camps. Since the rush hour brings to mind the Nazi atrocities, it is of necessity important. *I think of the way the Jews were herded into the cattle cars* is also an example of reported thought. In addition, the expression itself is something of a cliché along with *I just panic* and *everything in me just freezes up.* Far from diminishing their effect, the very set nature of the phrasing, found seldom in her telling, reinforces the speaker's point. Her final sentence, *It's just as dehumanizing,* continues the animal motif first detected in *herd* and *cattle car,* giving an impression of a more general metaphor of beastliness. *Dehumanizing* itself is an interesting lexical choice, notable for its formal, almost scientific tone.

The essence of Proposal 3 is that during rush hour in the subways people are so deprived of their basic needs of air, space, and individuality that they become like beasts.

B obviously does not accept that the speaker's story demonstrates that people were dehumanized by the conditions in the subway, causing the speaker to faint. On the contrary, she asks the speaker:

B: But people were pretty nice, hm?

She does not indicate that she disagrees with any of the presuppositions of Proposal 3, but merely that she did not believe that the facts recounted by the speaker justified characterizing those who ride on the subways during rush hour as *dehumanized*. The adversative conjunction *but* and the request for an answer indicated by *hm* leave the teller no choice but to debate whether people were indeed nice. Proposal 4, *People are nice,* relies upon the information in the speaker's own story detailing the concern of strangers on the crowded subway:

A: then all of a sudden there was a lot of space and . . . people . . . helped me up, and . . . someone set me down . . . . and then . . . someone took me off . . . the car, . . . and he got a policeman . . . and he came over . . . and asked what was wrong and he asked me just two questions . . . and he sat me down, and they got an ambulance, . . . and the ambulance came, and took me to . . . a nearby hospital.

All of these are the actions of people acting properly toward a stranger, being *nice,* in a word.

The speaker's answer to B's Proposal 4A is very ingenious. Far from denying that people were *nice* as shown prima facie by her own story, she accepts that they did, in fact, *act* in ways which were *nice*:

A: People . . . are . . . ALways nice when there's a crisis like that

but she goes on to deny that they were *really nice*:

A: And . . . the context was right . . . I was WHITE, . . . I was a young woman . . . I was we-ll dressed, I was obviously not a pervert, or a deviate, . . or a criminal . . . HAD I BEEN . . . had I been . . . anything OTHER than that . . . I could've fallen . . . and they would've stepped OVER me . . . or perhaps ON me.

Since stepping on people who are not white or well dressed, or even failing to extend help to everyone, is not being *nice,* but is, instead, being "bigoted," which is quite opposed to "niceness," the speaker's answer solidly rejects B's proposal. The heightened stress leaves no question that the strangers were only *nice* because she was not other than what she was. The repetition of *had I been,* as well as the graphic description of a purely hypothetical situation in which she was *OTHER,* join with the large number of details of exactly what she was (totally acceptable) and what she was not (a despised member of society) to leave no question that for the speaker her story could not be taken as an instance of *People being nice.*

The speaker has a counterproposal, however. At the end of her long description of how *people are not really nice,* she suggests Proposal 5, *People are like that in New York:*

A: HAD I BEEN . . . had I been . . . anything OTHER than that . . . I could've fallen
   and they would have stepped OVER me . . . Or perhaps ON me. You know cause
   that's the way people in New York ARE.

We have already discussed most of the evaluation present in this portion when
discussing Proposal 4 above. Only the last line, *You know cause that's the way people in
New York are,* distinguished Proposal 4B from Proposal 5. Not only is this a story
about how people are not *really nice,* the speaker puts it forward as a story of how
people in New York really are. The stress on *are* and the appeal to the audience with
you know both highlight this sentence.

C insists in her Proposal 6, *The speaker is an inept subway rider,* that the speaker
may deviate negatively from the norm of American adults. Implicit in her question is
the notion that the speaker's story may well be an account of her incompetence as a
subway ride.

C: Didn't you used to grab the strap in the subway?

is C's devastating phrasing of her proposal. The locution *grab the strap* is, itself, an
indication of C's mastery over the subway idiom and probably over the subway itself.
Her use of the doubting negative interrogative *didn't you used to* gives the impression
that C has thought very little of the speaker's whole story, since she might not have
fallen at all if she had been a competent traveler—a proper, responsible adult.

The speaker's answer to C's charge of incompetence is to move back into the story
proper, return to the moment of fainting, and evaluate the altered perceptions she
experienced while losing consciousness. First she answers C's question:

A: I . . . was just saying . . . I . . yeah . . . But I was in . . . standing in the center of
   the car, holding onto the center POLE . . . and I just slid down the pole.

Since she was holding onto the pole, evaluated by increased stress and repetition of
the key word *pole,* she did not need to grab the strap even though she normally did.
Having re-established herself as a competent subway rider, she presents her last
proposal, 7, *Fainting warps perception,* to re-establish herself as a competent storyteller:

A: A-nd uh- . . . it was funny because . . . in my HEAD . . I said . . . my
   AWAREness was such . . . that . . . that that I said to myself . . . gee, well there's
   a PERson over there falling DOWN. And that person was me.

Here a variety of devices are present: the familiar heightened stress on important
words; redundancy of expression of important information that involves her consciousness (*in my head, my awareness was such*); and; as in Proposal 1, reported speech.
This time the reported speech is closer to direct than to indirect discourse—the *gee,*

well which precedes the substance of the sentence is a much more forceful and immediate way of noting that she commented on herself fainting than the earlier *I remember saying to myself*. Unlike the earlier rendition of the story, the fainting itself is curiously muted: *and I just slid down the pole*.

Although the speaker does not comment on why she thought she experienced something impossible (i.e. watching herself faint), she understands that her audience can interpret the marked evaluation on perception to mean that she merely *perceived* herself as experiencing something impossible. The expression *my awareness was such,* with its formal, scientific ring, perhaps makes this point most clearly. The external remark *it was funny because* shows that she agrees that what she perceived was odd. It also has the effect of eliminating any lingering remains of Proposal 1, that this is the story of a frightening experience. Proposal 7 suggests that this is the story of an interesting experience.

B accepts the proposal by saying:

B: It's weird.

and the speaker accepts the acquiescence and closes the negotiation by answering:

A: OK, that was . . . that experience.

After detailing a number of proposals, and looking at many minute aspects of the texts and declaring them to be "evaluative," it seems fair to ask if everything can be thought of as evaluative. Can a case be made that every part of a text contains a proposal of what the story is all about? In light of these reasonable questions, let us look briefly at the missing proposal, *Men Are All Like That*. This proposal could have been made during the long narrative portion in which the speaker is recounting her interaction with the policeman:

A: He came over, . . . and asked what was wrong, and he asked me just two questions. Are you pregnant? . . . To which I said no. I mean they . . . like he was told that I had fainted . . . And uh . . . uh he said . . . in a very embarrassed kind of way, do you have your period now. . . . And I said no . . . A-nd he said OK, and he sat me down, and they got an ambulance.

B apparently expected the policeman's embarrassed questioning of the speaker's "biologic functioning" to be of some import. Her chuckle, as if getting the point, when the speaker says *he was told that I had fainted,* becomes a full laugh with the question *Do you have your period, now?* But the speaker ploughs right on with her detailing of events.

Jefferson (1979) suggests that "tellers can propose and recipients accept that a response was premature, that there is more story to come, and that upon a next completion point, recipients have another opportunity to respond via their corrected understanding of the story" (p. 220). This comment is made in reference to a conversational fragment in which the speaker *explicitly* corrects a recipient's misunderstanding. What we have in this story and in some others we have looked at is an *implicit* correction of a misunderstanding in which the speaker strongly underevaluates an event or situation potentially worth evaluation and hurries on with the next part of the story.

In this case, the conversation with the policeman, normally a highly charged event, is reported in a very matter-of-fact way. One event follows another: *he said . . . I said* are events phrased in a muted form, indistinguishable from unevaluated events as *he sat me down* and *they got an ambulance.* He asked his question *in a very embarrassed kind of way* has some evaluative force, as does *like he was told that I had fainted* but somehow the force is lost, dissipated by the combination of the soft voice in which she details the events and the rather monotonous chain of simple declarative sentences in the past tense filled with details of a rather pedestrian sort. A story about how a policeman asks a woman embarrassing personal questions he could never ask a man is the kind of story which has very strong narratable qualities, especially in a group of somewhat feminist women. That she did not choose to make *men are all like that* or *Man's inhumanity to woman* one of her proposals, is perhaps due to a possible plan to make a more global and important point by asserting that subway travel is inhuman and even "dehumanizing." But this is the most idle sort of speculation. We cannot know what the speaker had in mind, by choosing not to do something which might never have occurred to her to do.

3.8 CONCLUSION

Some people have asked if these stories are anomalous texts. After all, not every story is so full of comments and interruptions, negotiations and discussion. However, real texts, collected from real speakers, are almost invariably complex. Stories told in unstructured conversation are often discussed, corrected, edited, amplified. The point of a story often changes in the course of narration, and afterward, even beyond the confines of the particular conversation in which it was told. Any point which is accepted as the point by all members of a group has to satisfy several constraints: the story must illustrate the point; the point must be of a narratable sort; and the point must be of interest to the members of the community who generate and receive it.

4.

THE WORLD EVOKED BY
AMERICAN STORIES

4.0 INTRODUCTION

If stories are complex, storytellers are that much more complex; if the storyworlds built by tellers in their stories are complex, the everyday world in which those tellers live and talk and interact with one another is that much more complex. Having looked at the linguistic structure of American stories and dealt a bit with the relationship between stories and embedding conversations, let us now turn our attention towards the tellers of those stories and more specifically towards the system of notions, ideas, concepts, and values which taken together form our common world view. The aim of the present enterprise, then, is not mainly to explain the stories which have been analyzed to "find out what they mean" but rather to explore the world which they evoke.

4.1 METHOD OF ANALYSIS

Taking as a point of departure those aspects of the stories which the narrators have evaluated as especially important, I will begin by inquiring what is interesting about them. I will ask that question in order to elicit from myself what is the most obvious, automatic, trite thing to say about "friends," for example, or "food." And then I follow where the discussion leads. Some constructs will appear very rich, while others may be exhausted sooner. In general, discussions will grow longer as the chapter unfolds because earlier elaborations of some constructs are available for further exploration. Not every facet of every issue can be discussed since the very basic presuppositions underlying American life are the focus of attention. Some will be hit upon repeatedly, however. The discussion will largely focus on "the individual," his "needs," "choices," "social responsibilities," and "interpersonal relationships."

Travel from one construct to another is accomplished by means of associative chaining. It is not really possible to talk about the "rights" of the individual without speaking, too, of his "responsibilities," or to inquire into "courage" without considering why one should not act like a "coward." I will try to be as self-referential as possible, looking at what I have just put forward as obvious and examining it to see what sorts of obvious statements can be made about *that*. I shall not try to come up with "new insights." Indeed, the success of this venture depends on the *lack* of novelty about the information unearthed. If I say something new, something controversial, I am probably expressing my own opinions and idiosyncratic, although culturally constrained, points of view. Since the aim is to get at the most globally acceptable remarks, the more conventional and stereotypic the attitude expressed, the more it reflects commonly held attitudes.

Those attitudes need to be explored, to be expounded, because they are commonplaces for Americans but for those to whom Americans are "foreigners", these clichés may well be very strange. Cultural differences are most strikingly observed in the most commonplace ideas about life.

From time to time, I will use excerpts from a particularly American genre of popular psychology and sociology books—the "how to run your life and know how to feel and relate to other people" book. These books are guides for living life "right," having the appropriate feelings, and expressing them in the best way to be "a winner in the life game" (T. I. Rubin, 1967). Most of these books discuss friendship or marriage but all take as their point of departure the individual person who is isolated and feeling helpless. Their advice is intended to help the individual feel competent, capable of "having relationships," strong, and "autonomous," while accepting that the "truth" of the human condition is that each human being is, quite deeply, alone.

The titles of the quoted books encode a wealth of culturally salient information:

- Actualizations: You Don't Have to Rehearse to be Yourself by Stewart Emery (1978)
- A Guide to Successful Marriage by Albert Ellis and Robert A. Harper (1977)
- Friends: The Power and Potential of the Company You Keep by Jerry Gillies (1976)
- Creative Intimacy: How to Break the Patterns that Poison Your Relationships by Dr. Jerry A. Greenwald (1975)
- The Adjusted American: Normal Neuroses in the Individual and Society by Snell Putney and Gail J. Putney (1964)
- How to Take Charge of Your Life by Mildred Newman and Bernard Berkowitz (1978)
- The Winner's Book by Theodore Issac Rubin, M.D. (1967)

A proper American, it seems, is adjusted, in charge of life, successfully married, a winner who knows how to have friends, stay free of poisonous relationships, and is himself.[1]

The purpose of using these "how to" books is not to substantiate that what I say is the truth about the way which human beings are, but rather to demonstrate that the presuppositions about the way the world is and the way people are which are stumbled on as I follow the threads of my intuition are not really personal statements. Well meaning, serious people who try to explain how the world is use exactly the same sorts of statements and rely upon exactly the same kinds of presuppositions about the world that we are trying to track down. For the same reason, sometimes I will use a line from a popular song, a proverb, or cliché. These are so "true," so "ordinary", that we hardly notice that they carry with them and evoke little pieces of a complex and extraordinary everyday reality.

Clearly, considering the enormity of the task, I will not be able to put together a very complete picture of that reality. This discussion of cultural constructs should be taken as only a demonstration of a method for using story materials as an entry into the cluster of interwoven ideas which support our daily lives.

I cannot prove that only a limited number of "interesting" things to talk about exist in a given culture, but that may well be the case. In working through various propositions from the Adequate Paraphrases and the proposals for meaning from "Fainting on the Subway," previously mentioned constructs will often re-emerge. In general when that happens, the discussion will take a new direction so that as many associative pathways as possible can be explored. In the last section of the chapter when we turn to "The Robbery" the aim will be to demonstrate as far as possible the redundant nature of these explorations and to sketch out how the discussion might have developed had those paths been explored earlier. A good deal of redundancy is to be expected in this sort of analysis since a large set of beliefs about the world would have little utility in structuring our experience.

In general, as has often been said, stories are about deviations from expected norms, although they often function as well to confirm the correctness of preconceived ideas about the way the world is. This fits very well with notions of the need for coherence and consistency in the world. Stories give us information about the way the world is—either how we expect it to be or how it differs from our model. The analysis of stories and speakers' motivations presented here similarly depends upon an assumed need for human behavior to be predictable—to conform to norms. My premise is that without the ability to model the interests and world-knowledge of others, human beings would have no idea of what to tell a story about. Indeed, in an

---

[1]Throughout this discussion, unless I am specifically dealing with women, I will use the male forms, "he", "his" etc. In part the English language still demands that we do so. To use "She/he", "his/hers" and the other compromise forms, merely makes the "solution" too obvious. There is a deeper issue here as well—the "unmarked" person is male, just as he is healthy, of normal intelligence, competent in common living skills, etc., as shall be developed in Chapter Five below.

incoherent universe, stories and other forms of communication would have little purpose. (See discussion throughout this chapter for analysis of some of the presuppositions rampant in this paragraph)

4.1.1 IN DEFENSE OF THIS METHOD OF CULTURAL ANALYSIS

Using American stories to tell the American story is an ambitious enterprise. Through the wide-ranging, almost uncontrolled expansion of the points of the stories which we have been looking at, we may find some American answers to some important (American) questions:

- Why are these ambitious questions?
- Why is it all right to be "ambitious"?
- Why do we want to know the answers to questions?
- Why is it important to know things in general?
- How do we select what is worth knowing?
- What is important? What is unimportant?
- What are people like?
- How do different sorts of people differ from one another?
- How should people behave?
- How is the world organized?
- Is the world organized?
- What is the world like?

It is fair to ask at this point why one would look to intuitive free association, starting from the "points" of conversational stories for the answers: Why base conclusions on the clichés of quack media healers instead of on the research of responsible psychologists, sociologists, and anthropologists?

And there are several answers to these questions.

In the first place, there has been surprisingly little work done on "world view" of developed Western cultures. Or, rather, there has been a great deal of work done but it is not called "science," it is called "philosophy", "aesthetics," and "ethics". Rediscovering "truth" in strings of clichés and best–selling advice allows us to examine it more critically and to discover the interconnections among basic values. We do not reach "absolute primitives" by this method; we reach a set of mutually supporting and defining constructs. These can then be isolated and the formal relationships among the elements specified.

Of course social scientists have done a great deal of detailed work on specific issues and problems in Western societies, particularly on American society. A close examination of both popular and academic psychological, historical, sociological, and anthropological literature reveals, however, that the "experts'" analyses and arguments are built upon exactly the sort of presuppositions which we are trying to reach. Often analysts will stand on one presupposition to examine others, just as I am doing. In this study, an examination of the shifting presuppositions is explicit as is the awareness of the role played by cultural presuppositions in both the form of the analysis and its presentation.

Clearly, I am a relativist—of the worst kind from the point of view of those who believe in universals, objectivity, explanation, *the* facts. But when we consult the experts, we find no more objectivity in their texts than elsewhere, no matter how the presentation may bristle with formulas, charts, statistics, complex syntax, or technical jargon. And though it is seldom admitted publicly (except in the pages of the *London Times Literary Supplement*), social scientists often find that the scholarship of "foreign" colleagues provides revealing insights into the authors' cultural background as well as possibly adding to the understanding of the subject matter at hand. For this book, there should be no conflict; the author's cultural background, although not her idiosyncratic experiences or viewpoints, *is* the subject matter.

Let us now turn to the stories themselves once again to see what can be learned about their tellers' world view from one American analyst's naive cultural exploration.

4.2 "FAINTING ON THE SUBWAY"

Since it is perhaps the most complex story treated, as well as the most recent, let us begin our exploration of American world view by examining, in turn, each of the Proposals for Meaning from "Fainting on the Subway". The aim is not to explain the story, nor to come to a decision of what that story was "really about" or "really accomplishing." Rather each of the proposals themselves shall function as mini–texts to be expanded. Many of the points explored in the expansion of these proposals will surface again in analyses of subsequent stories. The proposals are discussed in the order in which they occurred in the telling. They are listed below to make reference easier.

Proposals For Meaning

1. Fainting on the subway is frightening.
2A. Personal problems in the past are important.
2B. Personal problems in the present are even more important.
3. Rush hour is as terrible as living through Nazi concentration camp horrors.
4A. People are nice.
4B. People aren't <u>really</u> nice—they are bigots.
5. People are like that in New York.
6. Speaker is an inept subway rider.
7. Fainting warps perception.

Fainting on the Subway is Frightening

Why is fainting frightening? and why is something frightening narratable? Fainting is frightening because it involves a loss of consciousness and hence a loss of control. If we are not in control, we cannot protect ourselves from danger, but are helpless, reduced to the status of children who must be cared for. Indeed, when the speaker faints, she finds herself in such a helpless state. She ceases to be in control of her own life but becomes someone to be sat down, taken hither and yon, asked questions, and left to *just stay* in a hospital. Not to be in control, to be unable to make decisions for ourselves, puts us at the mercy of other people, which is extremely frightening. An adult trusts only himself to know what to do, and, ultimately, to act in his own best interests. Fear in general is an interesting topic for a story, because it is painful and confusing. People are supposed to be happy and unafraid, yet fear is often justified. Knowing when to be afraid is one mark of an adult. Tension can be created in stories which involve fear because there is always a question of whether that fear will be shown to be justified; fearing unnecessarily makes us children; not fearing when there are grounds for fear is a sign of madmen or fools.

Personal Problems in the Past Are Important

In the story the speaker details a number of factors which added together produced a state of *tremendous emotional pressure*. But why detail these circumstances at all? No doubt she felt it necessary to make it abundantly clear that she was not the sort of person who normally faints; she usually functioned properly unless there was a compelling reason to do otherwise. But why are such personal problems of interest? Americans find information about people to be endlessly fascinating. Even Europeans, closer to us culturally than many other peoples, are often struck by how often Americans will offer details of emotional or personal situations to even a casual acquaintance.

We value openness, and the closer the individual is to us, the more interesting his personal affairs. But, why? Perhaps because the individual is all-important. Concern with the individual is the center of our political, judicial, religious, and economic philosophies. We bring our children up to be able to act independently. Our heroes are men who stand against the crowd. We have few set rules of conduct, of how to be, but many meta-rules of each finding our own way. Information about other people's difficulties gives us information about how to act in our own lives; seeing how others deal with adversity gives us a model for dealing with difficulties of our own; and learning of someone else's hardships and failures makes us feel more "normal," less inadequate, since we know that we ourselves cannot deal perfectly with every situation which comes along either.

An adult must be strong, able to manage for himself, and each of us knows that we cannot. This is a dilemma, a problem facing us because of our deepest feelings about the way adults are and how they ought to be. We are very concerned with our own individuality, and yet we are preoccupied with being popular—we must each be unique, but not odd, different. Someone who confides to us his personal problems makes us feel trusted. It is a way of baring the neck. By discussing her problems, the speaker in "Fainting on the Subway" simultaneously announces that she is vulnerable and that she is unafraid, that she is "normal" and that she is "unique." One way that her recital declares her normalcy is in the exact choice of details selected to show her distress: she had no air; she had insufficient room; she had not eaten; she had no job, and, presumably, little money—all needs which we take to be "basic human needs."

As one popular psychology book puts it:

> Whatever else man may be, he is first of all an animal with certain requirements for oxygen, tolerable temperatures, water, sleep, food and so forth. (Putney and Putney, 1964, p. 22)

If those requirements are not met, a human cannot survive and thus an adult cannot behave like an adult. That needs are not always met may mitigate the responsibility of an individual to perform adequately. Although an adult must be strong, competent, always in control, this is not possible if basic needs are not met. This argues for a physical, materialistic view of the world: being deprived of "needs" is an excuse for not behaving as one should (see Benedict [1967] and Goffman [1961] for extended discussion of the "needs" of human beings in Japan and the United States respectively and the results of depriving them of those "needs").

Personal Problems in the Present Are Even More Important

In proposing that her problems in the past have ramifications for the present, the speaker relies upon the audience's understanding of the nature of "needs" and the explanatory power of personal history. In addition she marshalls the very significant power of the immediate experience of an individual. If past problems are fascinating, present ones are that much more so. By stating that she is still unable to ride a subway alone, a totally normal and everyday act for many people, she relies on a group of cultural presuppositions to carry the force of her comments.

Each individual has a unique history, and events and experiences in a person's past can account for personality and behavior in the present. Unlike many other peoples who ascribe the way a person is to the events surrounding his birth or the nature of one's ancestors, we have a causal and historical explanation for the present state of an individual. By bringing the effects of this experience into the present, the speaker is bringing it closer to her audience—insisting that this is not merely a story about the past, but is, in fact, a story about the present and an explanation of why she is less than totally competent at carrying out the comings and goings of everyday life.

Rush Hour is Dehumanizing: Like a
Nazi Concentration Camp

We may ask why a story which could stand as an illustration of horrors equal to those of the concentration camp might be narratable? Since stories of atrocities are not necessarily to be found in all cultures, we cannot assume that it is "human nature" to be interested in horror; yet for us nothing is more tellable. Why?

Because to deprive someone of his needs is to treat him like an animal. An animal is without individuality, at the command of instincts, without the faculties of language or thought. To treat a person as an animal is to transform him into an animal. The worst fate which can befall someone is to become like a beast; and the worst pain one person can inflict on another is to reduce him to the animal. Nazi concentration camps and, presumably, New York subways, epitomize the way the world should not be and thus a story about these matters is an illustration of a strong deviation from a proper world.

People Are Nice

Stories are often built around deviations from expected norms of behavior, of "the way it is supposed to be," as can clearly be seen in Proposal 3. However, stories can also be moral tales of right conduct, or tales which illustrate the proper and the true. People are supposed to be "nice" and help each other in difficult situations. This type of kindness toward strangers is built upon the very strong democratic and pragmatic notion that each individual should be treated equally, especially when he cannot help himself—after all, anyone might be in a similar position someday. Whether stranger, friend, or kinsman, someone who needs help must be aided. In American culture, the primary bond between individuals is by virtue of their common humanity, not, as in many cultures, between those who have formal relationships with one another by reason of family, clan, or social position, although such ties are, of course, recognized and are very important.

We are all more alone than is possible for someone with closer ties to imagine. Friends, family, teachers, religious leaders—all are temporary relations at best. American "how to" books extol the importance of the individual freeing himself from ties which are too binding, too restrictive.

> To view all your friendships as temporary, as unfeeling as this may seem to you, will actually enhance the quality of those relationships, make them more human. For our lives are temporary things, and to cling, to hold on, is foolish as well as self-defeating. (Gillies, 1976, p. 200)

Any given person may be a potential "friend" and any given situation may be one in which one makes the kind of ties which render us less alone. Being "nice" is a way of keeping our options open. By helping and being helpful to people regardless of the degree of relationship we have to them, we have the possibility of developing a relationship to them. However, we must not allow ourselves to be overwhelmed by our desire for companionship:

> If you are a healthy and mature individual, you will acknowledge that other people are necessary to your growth and existence. If you are a needy, dependent individual, you will be desperately seeking others to reaffirm you, to love you, and however many people become a part of your life, it will never be enough. (Gillies, 1976, p. 148)

Thus, there is a basic and often painful conflict between the need for friendship, ties, community, and the very strong pressure to be an individual who is self-contained and responsible only to himself.

People Are Not Nice

The speaker counters the proposal that "people are nice" by insisting that they were not *really* nice, but were nice to her only because she was the kind of person anyone would be nice to without having to be a nice person through and through. This comment is based on the assumption that it is possible *to act* one way, and *to be* another. Being is rooted in what is really felt, not what is merely done. Thus it is possible to know someone's true nature apart from his behavior. This is quite a novel notion to many non-Americans, who wonder how one can know this true nature exists, if there is no manifestation of it in behavior.

That people may be one way "inside" and show a very different face to the world is a psychological commonplace. The "outer" face is felt to be less genuine, less "true" in important ways. By acting in accordance with the outer face and not the inner face, a person does an injustice to himself and ultimately to others who are not relating to the "real" person. This "real" person exists, however, and is most readily accessible in moments of great emotion when the "true" person may be liberated from the "falsely behaving person." American psychotherapy is based on getting to know and liberating the "true" person through techniques which induce, encourage, permit, and reward outbursts of anger, pain, rage, and sadness which are "more genuine" than the rational, intellectual, controlled, socially pleasant reactions which are normally encouraged and required.

This deep, emotional, "true" self is always lurking and it *is* the true self, the one which emerges when there is a threat to the individual. It is therefore imperative for people to keep tabs on the true selves of others—because in an emergency the true self will be present, complete with the "real feelings" and the rational "outer" self will be gone. When the speaker insists that the subway riders were not "really nice" she refers to the knowledge every adult must have that the world is not as it may seem, people are not as they seem, not even as they behave. People are what they would be under the most trying circumstances. When you can trust someone "when the chips are down" you can trust him. It is important to be able to distinguish between what a person may be like under pleasant conditions from what he might be like when things get difficult.

People Are Like That in New York

Why are New York stories interesting? New York and New Yorkers are quintessentially "other" for most Americans, including New Yorkers. Anything can happen in New York, and it will probably be more exciting, more interesting, and worse than anything which happens anywhere else (unlike Texas, where things are only bigger and better). Even a story documenting how New Yorkers are ordinary folks who can do a stranger a kindness is narratable because such a story is an atypical New York story. The deviant case is always interesting; and New York is a deviant part of America, in marked contrast to the Midwest, which is the American norm.

Why is the deviant so fascinating? The everyday so humdrum? The exception is so exciting because it presents new possibilities, shows new vistas, gives an indication of a world in which the traditional encumbrances are not felt. The different, the deviant, the exotic is interesting because it represents a type of freedom. The individual experiences himself as more fully individualized, more in touch with inner capabilities, unfettered by tradition, *free*. Freedom unfettered, independent, able to experience the possibilities of the world, to understand its complexity. These are all self–evident goods. Therefore, we are always fascinated by the deviant, although often frightened and disapproving of it. We take great pains to try to establish the "norm," if only to show how *we* do not fit it. (Even the discussion of evaluative functioning and cultural salience is built on the idea of norms and the power of deviance from norms.)

Speaker an Inept Subway Rider

A story of ineptness is fully narratable because adults are supposed to be competent, to be able to take care of themselves, and to be knowledgeable about their environment and the ways of managing everyday aspects of daily life. Failing to control the environment, being unable to "cope," is shameful. Difficulties with the environment, other people, or even with oneself, can be dealt with, can be overcome, but only with knowledge. Knowledge is power and control. Adults are knowledgeable; children are ignorant. The most stigmatized in our society, the mentally retarded, are pitied and despised because they alone among humans can never be "adult," never be "competent," never "know."

One requirement of adults is that they "manage" their lives. Our lives are a kind of work to be done well, like any other type of work. To live incompetently is synonymous with living "wrongly." An incompetent person, like any other stigmatized person, makes "normals" uncomfortable and his presence in the collective is barely tolerated. A person who is unable to DO is excluded from life because his presence is unbearable and because a person who suffers is wrong. Suffering in itself is a sign of wrongbeing. (See Goffman [1963] for a discussion of "stigmatized" and "normal" persons. These are his terms.)

We live in a hierarchical system of inherited prestige and power, a system in which relatively few privileged persons share in the tremendous wealth and policy-making institutions of the world's richest nation. Yet our professed belief is in the equality of all men before the election officials who control the ballot box, before the police and judges who administer the laws, before the laws of chance and fortune, and before God himself. In fact, we have no alternative but to maintain that all men have equal chances of becoming the election official, policeman, or judge, though we temper this equality by insisting that "each man gets what he deserves" through the workings of chance and the movements of the Lord.

By postulating that only those who "deserve" them get the goodies, we attempt to combine two obvious and irreconcilable "truths"—everyone is equally entitled to wealth, power, and good fortune, but not everyone ends up with an equal share. Those who don't end up on the top of the heap obviously don't deserve to. One does not deserve to succeed if one is guilty; therefore, failure to make money, have political power, or even good health is a punishment for some unspecifiable wrongdoing on the part of the individual. Faced with the unavoidable fact that some rich or powerful people are not morally pure, we assume that those people suffer, too. They must feel guilty and be unable to truly enjoy their ill-gotten gains. Unable to look at themselves in the mirror, they are in pain, too, which "proves" their sinfulness and preserves the integrity of the "suffering equals sin" system.

Since one gets what one deserves, people who are suffering are getting their due. Suffering equals sinfulness, and sinfulness is necessarily accompanied by feelings of guilt which are themselves painful. Psychoanalysis and the Judeo-Christian religions both operate on this unhappy principle. Political and financial power is concentrated rightly in the hands of those who are not themselves oppressed since an oppressed person is guilty of suffering, at the very least, and is therefore unworthy of having any political power or asserting himself forcefully enough to demand that his unequal lot be improved. The oppressors are less compromised by their participation in an oppressive situation than the oppressed. Those in authority are "more equal" than their social inferiors; the elite has proven its worthiness to rule by the mere fact of having succeeded in being in command. If it were not worthy, it would not have succeeded. The stigmatized, therefore, can be seen as subversive as well as immoral. They undermine the system of political control by their very helplessness and the fact that we must accept the fact that their fate is not, in fact, their fault. We know that the unfortunate may well be innocents, people like ourselves whose plight is not a punishment for wrongdoing but merely an accident of fate, something which could happen to anyone. Those who cannot DO stand at the center of a complex set of mutually exclusive, deeply held beliefs which are very close to the core of our thoughts about the way the world is—how it makes sense.

A world which makes no sense is considered unbearably painful. Anthropology, cognitive and interpersonal psychology, even physics and chemistry depend upon deeply held beliefs about the coherence of the universe. Societies attempt to structure the world for its members, much as a creature's sensory apparatus acts to arrange the stimulus from the outer world into patterns which can be processed. Children are seen to be structuring their world as they grow and learn—autistic children, however, may suffer from an inability to structure sensory input and therefore live in a world which is incoherent and thus overwhelming, frightening, and paralyzing. The quest for scientific knowledge is said to spring from a similar need to make an otherwise intolerably complex and inchoate world into a whole in which it is possible to be safe because it is possible to know, and to understand which causes lead to which results. An organism which cannot predict, we are told by psychologists, cannot survive. We believe in predicting; we plan, we compare the past to the future using the present as a bridge between the events which we believe have happened and those we are sure will happen. To be disoriented, to be unable to understand, to be unable to create meaningful patterns is perhaps the worst fate which can befall a person because a person who is disorganized *knows* that he is disorganized and cannot function. At the bottom of this discomfiture is the belief that people are by nature conscious beings who must be in control of their environment. To be at the mercy of uncontrollable forces is unbearably destructive for the individual because they render him helpless and thus unhappy.

Being "happy" is, of course, a self-evident good. The popular sociology book, *The Adjusted American,* defines happiness as "the emotional state that accompanies need satisfaction" (Putney and Putney, 1964, p. 16). While most of us would probably define "happiness" somewhat more in terms of enjoyment, not needing anything, but also feeling "good" about what is happening, happy is what people are supposed to be, what they have a right to be—at least some of the time—if they are living correctly. Indeed, since people are supposed to be happy, not being happy is a sign that things are not as they should be. Other people observing someone being unhappy may feel compelled to find out what is wrong and to try to change the situation so that the unhappy person re-enters the normal and desirable state of happiness. Therefore, failing to be happy when there is no reason not to be happy is actually not proper behavior since other people might have to act in order to change the situation and the person's mood from an unpleasurable to a pleasurable one. This is one reason why there is so much emphasis on smiling, since by smiling people signal that they are happy, i.e. there is nothing wrong which anyone else should do anything about ("When you're smiling, the whole world smiles with you").

Naturally, there are a number of assumptions involved in statements such as "people would want to do something about unhappiness to change it to happiness." First of all, it must be understood that people are capable of acting individually to change things and that there is a positive obligation on the individual to be helpful (i.e. effect positive change) whenever possible. This ties in with pitching in in an emergency, or helping a stranger who looks lost find his way. Since people need people and any person can extend help to any other person, one of the best ways to make someone else happy is to be friendly, i.e. act as a friend would under the circumstances, although the individuals concerned may not actually be in a friendship relationship to one another. Since friends are pleased to be with one another, a big smile is one of the surest ways of making a stranger feel at home, or someone in distress feel better, because it is clear that he is "among friends" whether with friends or perfect strangers.

Someone who remains unhappy—and fails to react to "being cheered up" by "acting happy"—despite the efforts of others to make him feel better, has to have a very strong reason for remaining gloomy. People have the capacity to change their own moods as well as to bring about change in others and to fail to "help yourself" and continue to be unhappy and thus force others to continue trying to make you happy is unreasonable behavior. Since the individual is supposed to do for himself, to fail to do so and to force other people to keep doing for you is the worst sort of "manipulative behavior." It is actually a form of shirking work since the unhappy person may be forcing others to do what he refuses to do for himself.

The aim of psychotherapy and other forms of psychological counseling is to help people be happy, often by refusing to allow them to continue to manipulate others—because once the individual knows what he is doing and how he is actually responsible for his own distress he will have no choice but to "get happy." It will then be clear that he is doing as much work in remaining unhappy and getting others to do for him as he would have to do for himself were he to "take charge of his life." Each person is responsible for his own life and for everything which happens in it and has the power to change for the better and thus the happier at any time he is willing to do the "work" of getting healthy. If you actually have to work as hard to be unhappy, and have to be guilty about being unhappy and shirking your work, you might as well give up being unhappy and be happy since it is no more effort—it doesn't cost you any more. And a proper person would obviously rather be happy than unhappy if he does not have to "pay more" for it.

There is no justification for a tragic vision of the world; if you are unhappy it is because you want to be unhappy—the world is, at worst, a neutral place and you make of it what you want to make of it. If you are unhappy, it is your own fault; if you feel yourself less than other people, a loser in the game of life, then it is your own fault and no one can help you but you can help yourself if you are willing to face pain (i.e., be courageous) to pay for your previous unhappiness.

Fainting Warps Our Perception of Reality

Altered perceptions are narratable because they suggest that the world may be somewhat different than we perceive it, or, at least, that we cannot always trust the evidence of our own senses. And if not our own senses, then what can we trust? Not the elders, not religion, not tradition, not fate; unlike many other peoples we rely upon none of these. Science? But science is built upon proof by experimentation, which itself is founded upon the ultimate authority: confirmation by the senses. If seeing is not believing, what can be believed?

We all know that it is impossible to be in two places at once. A story which says that someone experienced being in two places at once is clearly of interest. Adults know that the universe is rational and for every apparently aberrant event there is a "rational" explanation. Even when we perceive something which is patently impossible, we "know" that there must be some explanation somewhere in the known and knowable world. The material world is all that exists, and man can control his own world and be *safe* in the world, not prey to childish fears and ignorant misconceptions when he knows the simple physical laws of the universe.

"Safety" is a basic need of human beings. A child must be protected by its mother in order to live; a society must protect its members and give them the security they need in order to survive. Children must be taught very carefully that physical situations may be hazardous and that the world is unsafe. Knowing how to cross the street, how to light a match, how to get in and out of a canoe, might save a child's life. Fire safety is important. Overloaded circuits, naked wires and high currents are unnerving because "you can never tell" when an accident might occur. Inadequate wiring in a hotel properly causes more concern than the absence of a view or other aesthetic considerations.

Our world is a physical world; physical dangers are important and "real" because they cause harm, "real" harm to our bodies. Emotions, social relations, are less vulnerable, less important, less real. Aesthetics are a "mere" pleasant aspect of life and in no way commensurate with "harsh, physical realities." "Out of the body" experiences, trance states, even deep religious rapture are suspect because they are not real. We know that we have a body and it cannot levitate; it cannot be in two places at once; it cannot transcend the physical and operate in another realm. There is no other realm. We may have experiences which lead us to believe that we are experiencing another way of being. In fact, the "spiritual" is one of the needs of human beings since it provides a kind of coherence for phenomena we cannot otherwise classify (i.e. control) but no adult should take it too seriously, should sacrifice his own life (or worse the lives of those who depend on him) for otherworldly aims.

The speaker acknowledges that she experienced herself as being out of her body and that her experience is reportable because it is so clearly not the way life is. But she underwent this experience for perfectly understandable reasons. Since she did not in fact believe that she had actually seen herself but merely *thought* that she had, she managed to bring into play all of the power of our feelings about the physical world. Sending a double message, an ambiguous signal, she stated simultaneously that listeners should be interested in what happened because it was impossible and value and accept her as one of themselves for knowing it to be impossible.

4.3 "EATING ON THE NEW YORK THRUWAY"

Turning from "Fainting on the Subway," with its very complex negotiation structure and many points to the simpler "Eating on the New York Thruway," reveals many similarities in the cultural constructs underlying the two stories.

A number of aspects of the American's world must be dealt with in connection with this story in detail, including: food, a physical necessity of life; friends and the demands of friendship, social necessities of life; and competence and autonomy, two overwhelming necessities for successful human living. Each of these very large areas is suggested by the story in some way: food is the theme which introduces the story and which ties the story in with the previous discourse, while matters of friendship and competence arise from consideration of the behavior of the characters in the story itself. Friendship as a theme to be explored arises because of the relationship between the two women, Carol and Livia, while competence is suggested by the problems involving the coke and the restaurant employees.

A Story about Food

Carol introduces the topic of food at the very beginning of the telling when she announces her story to be *"about water or coke"* (Clause 33–34). Food is one of the pleasant necessities of life—eating communally is enjoyable and there is a wide diversity of foods good and tasty to eat.

For Americans, food is normally a safe topic of talk. Different eating habits are matters of interest, and though people are often categorized by their eating habits, they are seldom morally condemned for them. We are usually pleased with what we eat and are willing to experiment and try other foods, although there are some foods we do not eat. In common with most peoples we are not omnivores. We find people who eat insects, worms, grubs, snakes, cats, dogs, or some wild birds (among other foods) as nearly unpeople, as are people who eat their meat raw. Foods we do not like may be "disgusting" but eaters of such foods seldom are really "immoral" unless they eat beings with whom we are used to having personal relationships (i.e. household pets and other humans).

Food is one of the necessities of life and eating is one of the primary functions. Other basic activities, such as breathing and sleeping, are not very interesting unless we are discussing how we are unable to accomplish them. Elimination and procreation, on the other hand, are very interesting topics but are taboo to discuss in adult social conversation except in special circumstances. Food is not narratable simply because it is a necessity of life, or because it is something we find interesting but in general, talk about food is considered *safe*. In social interactions it is very useful to have some topics which are interesting to talk about, about which everyone has opinions, and about which there can be disagreement without serious social rupture.

Food becomes socially dangerous as a topic when it is linked with one of two other topics: economics or health. Everyone needs to eat, because people must eat to be healthy, and so the notion that some people cannot afford to eat is extremely upsetting. If they cannot afford food then they cannot live properly and not living properly, they are not responsible for what they do. Everyone in an equal and fair society should have the necessities of life or something is very wrong with the working of the system. The system must work or life becomes incoherent and thus impossible.

Depriving someone of food is immoral, although the taste of food and the nature of the food is not so important. Thus, it is right that poor people and people in prison eat unappetizing food, since the taste of food is a pleasure, but it is wrong if people have no food. Without the necessities of life, people die or become like animals.

Some food is not healthy and should not be eaten. Underdone pork is a health hazard, as is potato salad left out in the sun. Unpasteurized milk is also suspect and someone who would knowingly eat such foods is not a proper person. This concern with health and the healthiness of foods spawns a variety of opinions about what is healthy. One way youth rebels is to pick different food as being healthy than their elders and then to berate their parents and other older folks for eating unhealthily. Unpasteurized milk, for example, has moved from −healthy to +healthy, but eating what is "healthy" remains important.

"Water" and "coke," the two substances which figure prominently in "Eating on the New York Thruway are two of the most common and innocuous foodstuffs (in a socially conventional environment). The speaker's assertion that there was a story involving those drinks would fit smoothly into almost any conversation involving food. Had she mentioned "caviar and escargots," instead, there would have been more question as to how this story fit into the ongoing discourse. Since the topic at hand was eating on the Thruway and she mentioned two very common liquids, both easily procured on the highway at rest stops, the story fit easily and in a nonthreatening manner into the conversation.

What is This Story Really About?

Having investigated the matter of food, let us now turn our attention to the Adequate Paraphrase of "Eating on the New York Thruway" arrived at in Chapter Three.

> Carol was "poisoned" by sipping a coke prepared by weird incompetent people who worked at the restaurant on the New York Thruway. She was saved by Livia who had brought along (an otherwise mysterious) gallon of spring water.

Although it may seem a step backwards, the analytic process begins by decomposing the Paraphrase into its component parts. Each proposition can then be explored individually to see where it leads.

The "plot" of the story reduces to two events:

> Carol drank a poisoned coke.
> Carol was saved by Livia who gave her water to drink.

While the contextualizing information consists of:

> The employees of the restaurant who made the coke were weird and incompetent.

The warning against drinking the coke—all of Livia's vague remarks.

That Livia had brought along springwater.

We will begin with the first event:

A Story About Poisoning

Food is supposed to be reliable, safe, predictable, especially in the United States. A coke is the most ordinary of the ordinary, the most American of the American. A coke which is poisoned is a betrayal of one's trust in the system to provide what can reasonably be expected.

The key word in the last sentence is "reasonably," since some things clearly are "reasonable" and others "unreasonable." The unreasonable can be wished for, hoped for, or prayed for, but an adult accepts that there are limits to what he can expect to have. The reasonable is a person's due. If he behaves correctly, then he should get what is "reasonably" coming to him. Indeed, since one gets what is coming to one, not getting the reasonably expected is doubly unpleasant: one does not get what one expected and one's worth is measured by what actually happened. What actually happens is more "reasonable" than what did not happen, since the supposedly reasonable would have happened had it been *truly* reasonable. Carol was punished for not knowing what was reasonable. This story is a moral tale in that respect—she is educated about the nature of the world and her ideas of the reasonable in relation to food are realigned, uncomfortably. However, her friend acted as a friend should act, and the experience was thus not altogether negative.

About Friendship

In order to understand the force of the story (Carol was saved by her friend who gave her some water to drink), we need to investigate what "friends" are like and gain some understanding of how they relate to each other. We must understand, too, why giving a friend a drink of water when she was "poisoned" by a coke might constitute an "act of friendship."

Friends are people who like each other, who accept each other as they are, and who willingly help each other in troubled times and rejoice together in happy times. Friends, above all "make us feel they really like us, really respect and appreciate us" (Gillies, 1976, p. 13).

Although "a friend is someone who I know will be there when I need him to be there" (Emery, 1978, p. 153), a "real" friend, like a good parent, will not be totally supportive:

> . . . won't settle for your being less than . . . [you really] are and kicks you in the ass when your being represents a lie about the way you really are. (Emery, 1978, p. 150).

Honesty is the most important aspect of friendship. In a friendship one must be free to be who one is and to tell the truth even if it is hurtful to the other person—but only if the hurting is done for the other person's good.

> There are people who, under the guise of honesty, are always telling other people things that barb and hurt them. This is honesty used in the service of vindictiveness. (Rubin, 1967, p. 33)

So, a good friend is helpful and honest and supportive, managing to negotiate successfully the very thin line between helpfulness and hurtfulness when something in the friend's behavior is not as it should be.

But why have friends when juggling needs and honesty is so difficult? Because in a friendship one can be oneself, one need "play the least amount of roles possible" (as noted by L. Buscaglia in Gillies, 1976 p. 165). With friends one can talk; one can share experiences; one can overcome loneliness. People need people.

> The more impersonal our society and its institutions become, the more the individual feels alone, alienated and lost. . . . The person adrift in the world with no anchor loses his identity, the meaningfulness of his life and, eventually, his emotional and physical health. (Greenwald, 1975, p. 11)

One solution, according to Greenwald, is to become your own best friend. This solution is clearly rooted in the more ordinary solution to the problem of loneliness: have friends.

Clearly, one has friends because they are *useful:* friends fulfill a human need, not to be alone. "Having" friends is *healthy*. Needing to have friends, relying on one's friends heavily, however, is not good. It is in conflict with the healthy individual's ability to be independent and get along fine by himself.

> Warning: Beware of the person who sends the message implicit or explicit, "I want someone to take care of me." Chances are he or she lacks inner intimacy and feelings of stability and self-love. (Greenwald, 1976, p. 13)

It is important to *choose* one's friends carefully because:

> We invest a lot of time and energy in our friends. Time and energy exist for us in limited quantities, and we can't afford to waste much of either. (Gillies, 1976, p. 13)

It is important to make choices properly because what an individual wants or does can influence events, other people, perhaps the future of the world. Choices made by individuals determine what may happen. Choice is a *fact* and the action of the individual is all important. History revolves around individual figures who made decisions, took chances, perhaps changed the course of future events.

Choice is not only an option for an individual; it is a responsibility. A proper person is one who acts autonomously in his own best interests:

> Autonomy means the capacity of the individual to make valid choices of his behavior in light of his needs. To the extent that his choices are limited . . . the individual is incapable of autonomy. (Putney and Putney, 1964, p. 10)

An individual who is "incapable of autonomy" is not free. In the opinion of the authors of *The Adjusted American: Normal Neuroses in the Individual and Society* such a person is "neurotic." And ". . . neurosis which inhibits the fulfillment of needs . . . is . . . a threat to physical as well as mental health" (p. 17).

Health functions in this argument as a self-evident good. People who are not capable of choosing correctly and thus protecting their emotional and physical beings are not proper members of society. If they cannot take care of themselves properly they obviously cannot take care of others and fulfill their roles as productive persons. The individual is always the most important person in his own life, and one does best by what one cares most about:

> In doing for others, we are also involved in doing for self through the personal satisfaction derived from relating to others in this way. (Rubin, 1976 p. 42)

So, one takes care of one's friends, but they should not *need* to be taken care of. "Taking care of" involves being there, being helpful, and being honest. Doing the supportive thing which helps the other person in his life but doing these things because one *wants* to do them. Friends must both "be" friends and "act" towards one another as friends. Unfortunately, these two constraints may come into conflict with one another, since one must *freely* behave as a friend is *constrained* to behave by the force of conventions of friendship. If one is not behaving in accordance with one's *true* feelings, then one is not being a true friend, because with a friend one should be honest; if one is not being honest then the relationship ceases to be safe for either side, since the "true" feeling might leak out at any time and reveal that the behavior has been a sham. Dishonesty can be devastating to a friendship and all that the friends have invested in the relationship over the years may not be able to save it.

If there are problems or upsets among two or more friends, it may become imperative for all involved to "have a talk" to try to "reach an understanding." Sometimes it may take a number of conversations to "straighten things out." Eventually one or both parties to the disagreement might give up trying. In the latter case, the relationship may be considered to be either at an end or else less solid than it had felt before the altercation. Relationships often feel *more* solid, however, after a process of reconciliation than they had before the difficulty developed.

Explicit communication has great power to build "trust" in a relationship. Trust is overwhelmingly important in relationships in which each party knows that he has the power to end the relationship if it is not pleasing to him and knows, too, that the other partner in the relationship has the same power. Friendships, marriages, business associations, neighbor relationships, and family ties are always threatened by displeasure on the part of any one of the parties involved. The threat that a relationship may be terminated if it is not "straightened out" puts it into a class of problems demanding immediate attention. Problems are there to be solved; problems in relationships are to be solved by talking things out, expressing feelings to the other person, by being "real," uninhibited by social conventions, by expectations of "being nice" and by "letting it all hang out."

Until the problem is straightened out, the people involved are unable to relate to each other normally. Merely being "nice" in a social way is "phony"; we need to know what the other person really feels because only then can we feel safe, can we rest assured that we are behaving properly towards the other person. If the other is denying the relationship, intending perhaps to break it off, then behaving as if a relationship really existed would be uncomfortable, would make a fool out of the person who believed the other to be truly involved. A commitment by both parties to "talk it out," "work it through," indicates a commitment to continue the relationship, paying for it with the time and energy spent in arguing, explaining, and sharing an upset.

Knowing that the other cares leads to a sense of safety and security. One relaxes; one knows that the other cares also and one has usually learned something about the other in the course of the process of working it out. What is learned becomes a token of the worth of the relationship since a piece of intimate knowledge about someone else may be used against that person in other arguments.

Once they have established that the relationship will go on, the disputing partners need to agree on the version of the precipitating events they will agree to share so that, should the matter come up again, it will not be a threat to the relationship because all will know what to think of it. A consensus would have been reached. In the course of all the talk about the problem, and the problem relationship, the people involved express their feelings towards each other and about the way things are. When we do so, we find that our "real" emotions are essentially indistinguishable since we feel a common battery of them: pain, anger, sadness, alienation, joy, warmth, insecurity, and so forth. Deep down, then, we are basically all the same. This sympathy and security which develops from feeling at one with the other person leads to a resolution of the original conflict and a strengthening of the relationship itself. Having been through something together and being still willing to continue the relationship has proven that there is something important there after all. In his book *Actualizations: You Don't Have to Rehearse to be Yourself,* Stewart Emery puts this whole matter nicely:

> The truth about you and me is that we have fundamentally similar essences and different realities. The different realities enable the game called relationship to take place. And the experience of the similarity of essence allows the game called relationship to take place

without threat. You can have a lot more fun playing the game if you are not worried about the outcome. (Emery, 1978 p. 91)

Once we have discovered our similarity, our essential equality, we need not be afraid of the other but are free to "have fun" playing the game of "relationship." Naturally, when we tire of playing that particular game with that particular partner, the relationship is once again in trouble, because it has stopped being "fun," being "enjoyable," being "useful."

Sad as it often seems, friendships do end, and in fact they must end when they are no longer useful. Gillies quotes "Group leader Emily Coleman" as saying:

Make a clean sweep. Trim down your list of friends to those who really inspire you, and you'll find you have time and energy to seek new friends. (Gillies, 1976, p. 197)

Coleman's proposal is predicated on the idea of there being infinite opportunities possible in life. The individual's responsibility is to make the best of his time and "resources," to take advantage of as much as possible.

Friendship, then, is almost a kind of property. We can invest time and money in it, expect to get things out of it, and exchange worn out relationships for better ones. At the core of all of this is an individual trying to stave off isolation, for his health, if for no other reason, and attempting simultaneously to "have" as many relationships as possible. Friendships are, by nature, temporary. The individual must choose to have them and choose to continue to have them by agreeing to behave as a friend quite spontaneously. Relationships in general are transitory, freely chosen, and should last as long as they have utilitarian value:

We must let go of our family, our friends, even our life. So long as we cling to life as a permanent possession, it will not be as full as it can be. (Reid quoted in Gillies, 1976 p. 200)

Life, friends, family, it seems should be viewed as *temporary* possessions. Friends are better than family in some respects:

The reason for this is obvious. We choose our friends. (Streamer quoted in Gillies, 1976 p. 210)

Choice emerges over and over again in these discussions as one of the most important aspects of human life.

A Story About Friendship

Let's consider briefly two important inferences easily made from propositions explicitly stated in "Eating on the New York Thruway":

Carol drank a "poisoned coke" (From Propositions 83–84)

Livia, Carol's friend had warned her against all comestibles at the Thruway Restaurant (from Propositions 37–40/43 and 44).

Carol was "saved" by her friend giving her water to drink. Both Carol and Livia behaved as proper people. Carol did not heed Livia's advice because she did not understand it, and, as an adult, she had to make her own independent decision. Livia behaved properly both by warning Carol against danger and then by offering her the spring water when Carol was in "danger". She did not hold it against her friend that Carol had previously ignored her warning. Carol accepted Livia's help, thereby allowing her own distress to be relieved and allowing Livia to demonstrate friend behavior by helping her out of her difficulties. Both women emerged from the telling as proper friends and proper adults.

A Story of Competence

To finish up this discussion of some of the issues raised by aspects of "Eating on the New York Thruway", let's look closely at two highly evaluated propositions in Carol's telling:

The coke was prepared by weird incompetent people (who may have been insane or mentally deficient) [Propositions 61–7/69/70/73]

Livia had brought along a gallon of spring water. [Propositions 39/44.]

The restaurant personnel were incompetent and Livia was competent.[2] They did not know how to do the simplest thing required of them, while Livia was well prepared for the exigencies of Thruway eating.

Adults are supposed to be competent. They should be able to take care of their own needs, as we have mentioned above, and they must be able to deal adequately with their environment. Without the ability to fend for themselves, people are in danger since each person is alone in the social world. There is no cushion of social or family ties, no dependable world which protects the individual or satisfies his needs. Along with the right to choose and the need to choose to fill his own needs, is the inevitable necessity of taking care of himself in every way.

People ought to do things for themselves and "doing" can be fun. Some of the more exclusive vacation spots in the United States with guest lists limited to the wealthiest and most socially elite have only the most basic accommodations including

---

[2]There are clearly problems involved in analyzing oneself as a character in a story or as a participant in an interaction. However, as hopefully this analysis will make clear, there are compensatory benefits as well since some aspects of what is involved in the data being analyzed are clearly more accessible to the participants than to more "neutral" observers.

ice boxes, no heat, primitive sanitary facilities. Public officials and bank presidents clean their own fish, repair their own gasoline outboard motors, and take the car into town for a lube job. Their wives, meanwhile, supervise their own children, iron their own clothes, and make the beds in the cabin. At home, these same people insist that their children do chores, even if there are servants to supervise that the dishes are put in the dishwasher properly, or that the lawn edges are trimmed correctly. Children wash and clothe themselves at a relatively early age: signs of independent purposeful accomplishments are welcomed and even insisted upon. It is not uncommon for even very small children of under three years to "get themselves organized" in the morning.

"No one's going to do it for you, so you'd better do it yourself" is one of the maxims of daily life and *being able* to do for yourself is a matter of pride and a source of self-worth. Not everyone knows how to fix a car, of course, though it is a source of embarrassment should anyone find that out. Some work may sometimes be substituted for other work. The substituted work must be at least as difficult, preferably have unpleasant physical associations, or pay better. If one or the other of the first two conditions are met, one is not guilty of "laziness," "irresponsibility," or "shirking." If one can use the time to greater financial advantage, then, clearly, one should do the work which pays more over that which pays less, even if the less remunerative is something one ought to do. Thus, a woman doctor need not clean her own house since she would make much more money by working than she would spend for a housecleaner. On the other hand, she should certainly garden or do her stint at the day-care center lest she be thought of as someone who refuses to do her fair share of the work.

These matters tie in with the idea of how to be a responsible member of society and the very strong constraint to act of one's own free will to benefit the public good. The importance of being cooperative, of being a good team member and working well in groups is important. Individuals should pull hard for the group because what is good for the group will eventually "pay dividends" for the individual. Collective action is seldom good as an end in itself, but a cooperative system is necessary to permit the individual to do things which he could not do for himself.

Usually one has a choice of how exactly to be helpful, but circumstances sometimes force the choice. When a river is overflowing its banks and threatening the community, people must respond. In rural areas, most fire protection is rendered by volunteer firemen who choose to work without pay. At the scene of an actual fire, however, it is not uncommon to see people who would not *choose* to spend time fighting fires actually doing so. In an emergency, one should do what one can and take pride in being able to do a lot.

Thus, Livia behaved properly in the restaurant by tendering emergency aid to Carol—quickly giving her water to drink which she had brought along as a proper preventive measure against the food on the Thruway. Her competence shows the incompetence of the restaurant staff in its worst light. They were not called upon to do anything extraordinary. Rather, Carol suggests in her telling that they were unable to do their jobs because they were much less than proper people. Mentally retarded and "crazy" people who cannot do their jobs are excluded from the responsibilities of adulthood. Only someone who is not a proper person does his job inadequately. Not being able to perform one's work competently is a mark of great shame, since one is paid to work well. One is almost stealing to take money for a job one cannot do.

4.4 "THE BADDEST GIRL IN THE NEIGHBORHOOD"

"The Baddest Girl in the Neighborhood", also involves a "bad" person: the "baddest girl" whom the narrator was forced to fight, more or less against his will. The Adequate Paraphrase of that story, arrived at after long analysis, is as follows:

> The narrator hit the "baddest girl in the neighborhood" because he could not tolerate being bullied for having no money.

A Story about Standing Up for Your Rights

In order to understand why this story was tellable, we need to understand what is storyworthy about a bad girl, about fighting a girl and about fighting when one would rather not do so.

Let's take these various points in order and begin by asking what a "bad girl" is and why one could build an (American) story around one. Since the second question is easier to answer than the first, we will begin with it:

A Bad Girl

A story about a "bad" girl is narratable because it is illustrative of a *deviation* from proper behavior and thus demonstrates the expectations about proper conduct which speaker and hearer both share. The girl in the story is bad because she extorts money and candy from other children, threatening them with violence if they do not accede to her demands. She is blackmailing them, using their fear of being beaten up as a club to get them to do what she wants.

What is wrong with blackmail and extortion is that the strong must help the weak and not exploit a relative lack of power. Reminding someone of his inferiority, let alone preying on that inferiority, makes the inferior unhappy, takes away from his sense of self-worth, makes him feel less than a person since all persons are equal. Making someone feel bad is wrong because it hurts to feel badly and it is wrong to hurt other people, unless it is in their own interest. Extorting by threat of violence puts the weaker person in a box with no means of escape; his freedom of action and possibility of choice are very severely limited. Should he resist the extortion attempt, the violent repercussion will make him feel his powerlessness. Should he agree to the extortionist's demands, he is powerless by virtue of his capitulation since he would have shown himself to be too weak to stick up for himself.

Someone who refuses to resist the outrage to one's sense of worth which an extortionist's demand represents is not acting like a man. By refusing to stick up for himself, the weak person proves himself to be morally weak and therefore deserving of his fate. A morally correct individual will not give in to coercion even if the odds are heavily against him because to do so would be cowardly. What is narratable about fighting this bad girl is that the narrator is showing himself to be a proper person and not a coward.

Let us consider this question of cowardice for a bit. Rather than use a "how-to-live-your-life book" as a source of American wisdom on this score, let us look at part of a discussion of Tonga views towards cowardice taken from Colson's anthropological study of these people:

> Tonga imagination . . . provides other interpretations . . . [of valorous deeds] . . . They find no virtue in the last ditch defense and no shame in cowardice. . . . *they do not expect others to choose death as a protest against the force of an opponent or as witness to the rightness of a cause, or to court death or serious injury for reputation's sake.* (Colson in Beidelman, 1971, p. 23. emphasis added)

The last sentence gives some strong indication of an Anglo-Saxon view of cowardly behavior: giving into the odds, abandoning a worthy cause because the chances of success are slim, saving one's skin instead of facing danger. Why are these wrong?

Simply put, cowardly behavior reinforces the evil forces which oppress the weak. To refuse to give way before a strong enemy assures the enemy of some pain in his victory and may act as a deterrent for further oppressors. It is morally wrong of the oppressed to allow themselves to be subjugated, to accept less than equal status. Cowardly behavior acts against the common good and against the best interests of the individual, since giving in to oppression may result in an unnecessary victory. Underlying a rejection of cowardly behavior is a notion of optimism. Things may well improve and the valorous will share in the spoils, while the cowardly will be guaranteed defeat.

In this story, the narrator's decision to fight the baddest girl despite his slim chances of success signalled his understanding and participation in the norms of brave, that is, noncowardly behavior. His action was brave insofar as her strength was superior to his, and it was justified because his cause was right, or at least because her extortionist cause was wrong. Standing up for his rights was the action not only of a brave boy, but also of a proper person. To allow himself to be oppressed would have been bad for him since he would have lived in fear, while acting courageously might well have also had good social effect, though he does not say so. By refusing to give in to her demands, the narrator made a choice to defend his freedom of action and independence of behavior.

4.5 "THE ORDEAL"[3]

"The Ordeal," the opening story of the "Kate's Triumph" sequence, is also about "courage," the opposite of cowardice. Many of the themes in this story are redundant, built upon constructs which were discussed at some length in the examination of other stories.

So far, in this chapter, I have tried to "open out" the argument, to try to explore as many non–redundant aspects of the stories as possible. However, in the closing sections, dealing with "Kate's Triumph" and "The Robbery," significant redundancies are explored. This strategy is designed, in part, to close the discussion with a demonstration of the limited set of possible story materials available within a culture. Though considerably larger than the set we have found operating within these stories, in its most essential elements, the narratable set is relatively small.

"The Ordeal": A Story of Courage

"The Ordeal" takes place in the delivery room of the hospital in which Kate gave birth to her baby. As told, it is a story of pain, courage, and "spunk." Let us begin with the Adequate Paraphrase of the story:

> Despite a very long and painful childbirth, Kate asks the doctor a million questions. Although she has lost a lot of blood and is "almost dead" she still appreciates her doctor explaining unpleasant material to her in a "straightforward" way.

This paraphrase offers a considerable amount of culturally salient material suitable for exploration.

In general, "The Ordeal" is a story of courage. As such it is related to "The Baddest Girl," which is also about physical courage, although Kate triumphed over her own pain, while the narrator of the previous story confronted a human adversary. We need to understand why Kate's physical condition is worth reporting in order to understand why the asking a great many questions in such a state might be a suitable story. We will also discuss why Kate appreciated the doctor's straightforward explanation and why that appreciation might function as one of a story's points.

While facing an "enemy" might be painful and difficult, calling for a certain type of courage—a courage with strong social utility—facing one's own pain, physical or mental, calls for courage of a more personal nature. Why is it courageous to "face" pain? Because pain hurts and it is normal not to want to feel something that hurts. Only a "masochist" would rather feel pain than not feel pain; however, growing and

---

[3]Both "The Ordeal" and "The Robbery" are too long to deal with in their entireties; therefore only parts of the stories will be analyzed. The Adequate Paraphrases upon which these analyses are based are available in print elsewhere—"The Ordeal" in Polanyi 1978a, and "The Robbery" in van Dijk in press— and therefore will not be replicated here.

changing, both necessary and beneficial, involve pain. An individual who wants to "grow" must accept the pain involved. Therefore, pain must be borne but it must not be enjoyed.

Courageous people do not enjoy pain, but they bear it with fortitude, without making life unpleasant or difficult for other people. Thus, understanding how much physical pain someone is in provides a measure of that person's courage. Someone who "goes to pieces" over a splinter is a weakling; someone who cannot bear the pain of having a tooth extracted without an anaesthetic may well be acceptable; and a soldier who does not cry out when his leg is amputated on the battlefield while he is fully conscious is very courageous.

There are several issues raised by these observations. First one can cause other people distress by "making a fuss." Second, one can assess how much pain is warranted by various physical problems. Finally one has a right to be upset by the "discomfort." Why is being upset by one's pain something to need to have a "right" to? Because someone else's pain is painful to an observer. Therefore, someone who is in pain and shows that he is in pain himself inflicts pain. In order to inflict pain without being wrong, one must have the "right" to inflict it. Who can inflict pain on whom is very tightly circumscribed; in general, the strong can punish the weak with "just cause"—i.e. either to help the punished "learn" some lesson, or to "protect society" from wrongdoing. Someone can also inflict pain without onus if he cannot help himself from doing so.

Full adult human beings are sufficiently in control of themselves that they can prevent themselves from inflicting pain. Therefore, someone who inflicts pain without meaning to is, by definition, not acting correctly and is less than a full human being, and has forfeited full adult status by being unable to exert self-control. A child-abuser may not be legally responsible for his actions if judged to be "sick," but such a person is not a fully acceptable adult.

Someone who enjoys inflicting pain or watching others in pain is a "sadist," another sort of "sick," that is, "wrong," person. Since being in pain itself causes other people pain, a very strong taboo exists against "making a fuss" and causing other people pain. Even small children will often apologize for expressing their pain, crying out that they are sorry while protesting against the pain itself. Adults, too, often apologize to doctors or nurses for being overcome by pain as well as to their friends and relatives, who, being closer to them, are more vulnerable to being hurt by their distress. It is very interesting that pain and apology are so closely connected, perhaps due to the familiar and previously discussed association of pain with wrongdoing. Pain can be "mental" as well as "physical"—seeing someone else in pain hurts the observer, or should hurt the observer, since it is "callous" not to react to another's suffering. The pain for the observer is, of course, not physical, but mental pain. Mental or "emotional" pain is so well established that it is possible to get a divorce on the grounds of "physical or mental abuse" and to recover damages through court action for "mental anguish."

One suffers "mental pain" by being deprived of a nonphysical "need".

> Young children need . . . a certain amount of love and esteem, help and support from the persons around them if they are to survive well physically and develop sufficient self–love, self–esteem, and self–confidence to become healthy and effective personalities. (Ellis and Harper, 1961, pp. 30–31)

A child who does not receive love, will not become a "healthy" adult, and health is very important. Although one may disagree on what is healthy, no American would argue that being healthy is not important. Therefore, an argument such as this one is very potent indeed. A child deprived of love will be unable to develop "self-love, self-esteem and self-confidence" needed for a healthy, effective, competent self. And it is of overwhelming importance to nourish the self because no one else will care for someone who does not take care of himself.

> Remember, after a certain time in your life *whatever* gets done is up to you. [Emphasis authors'] (Newman and Berkowitz, 1977 p. 12)

Without the satisfaction of basic physical needs, a person will die. Basic non-physical needs such as love, acceptance, comfort, companionship, caring, help in times of stress or pain, all of which are satisfied by parents for their children, must be satisfied by the adult for himself. There is no one else. We are all really alone.

An adult must face life courageously, put up with pain in order to show self-sufficiency and not involve others unnecessarily in his pain. An adult knows that he is alone. Only "dependent," "sick," "wrong" people believe that other people are there to help them when they are in need. One's friends will help, of course, but only if we do not *need* help, but are merely in a position where being helped would be useful. Needing anything other than the self is "unhealthy," and needing the self is the basic tenet of human existence. Without a competent, strong, courageous self, one has nothing, one cannot survive.

Kate's spunk, her willingness and eagerness to ask a million questions despite her pain and loss of blood was an indication of her courage and her strong and positive attitude toward life. Since life is always changing, always new, and there are always possibilities for new experiences, it is imperative that the individual not succumb to inertia and avoid or evade exciting opportunities. Kate wants to *know* all about her world, to be in control of what was happening to her, and to make choices and decisions. She does not want to be a passive participant in her own life but a fully responsible adult. Her asking questions in such different circumstances in which there is no expectation of such active involvement indicates that she is the fully adult person she wants to be. The doctor's straightforward answers to Kate's questions, which detailed the unpleasant nature of her difficulties, demonstrated respect for Kate's praiseworthy and fully adult behavior. To deny someone knowledge is to insult that person, showing that he is regarded as not fully adult, not fully capable of accepting "reality." Kate's wholehearted acceptance of reality as evidenced by her enthusiastic response to the doctor's comments validates both the respect of the doctor and the respect of the recipients of her story—Kate is truly worthy of respect since not only did she withstand the pain and want to know insistently and courageously, but she also responded positively to what might have been thought of as unpleasant news. Kate can take it. Nancy and Susan, the protagonists and co-tellers of "The Robbery" may be less able to "take it" or what they were forced to "take" may be more than a proper person can manage.

4.6 "THE ROBBERY": A STORY OF FEAR
AND VICTIMIZATION

"The Robbery" is a long story with many points emphasized at different moments through the talk, including Nancy and Susan's ability to identify their assailants because of the auditory acuity of the one and the visual acuity of the other. At some moments, it is a story of competence, very much like the other stories in which control over experience is a central theme. However, strength and competence are only aspects of the story. If we look carefully and consider carefully all of the propositions in the storyworld and the various types of evaluation both through pseudo-conversation and other devices, we come to a much blacker picture. The explosive sound from the story recipients which greeted Nancy's remark about the gun being a foot from her head was not a sound of admiration for her courage but an expression of awe for the fear that encounter engendered.

Let us begin this final look at the world evoked through the stories analyzed in this book with the following Adequate Paraphrase of "The Robbery":

Susan and Nancy were very frightened because they might have been killed when they were robbed at gunpoint by people who will not be convicted.

If this Paraphrase is broken down into constituent propositions, the following list results:

1. Susan and Nancy were very frightened.
2. Susan and Nancy might have been killed.
3. Susan and Nancy were robbed at gunpoint.
4. The people who robbed Susan and Nancy will not be convicted.
5. The people who robbed Susan and Nancy were very frightening.

The first point which concerns being frightened was discussed earlier in the discussion of the meaning of Proposal I of "Fainting on the Subway." The second point, however, has not been explored specifically, although many of the analyses have touched on related issues.

Why is being killed frightening? There are two closely related reasons: one because it is frightening to die and the other because it is frightening to be forced to die prematurely, violently, and with full knowledge of the impending event.

It is frightening to die because dying represents the final abdication of control. Dying is the separation from the self and the ultimate helplessness without even a consciousness to deal with the helplessness and protect the self against it. Death is the end and the end is the ultimate horror. The gun which the robbers had, could have killed Nancy and Susan. The women's terror was appropriate when they felt fear at the presence of the gun.

Being robbed is upsetting even without the threat of extermination. Being robbed deprives a person of his possessions, reduces him to penury. Adults have possessions; with possessions, with money, they can care for themselves, take care of their own needs. Reduced to dependence by being penniless is a sign of weakness, of being unable to care for yourself. The poor man is punished for his wrongdoing by being poor. Susan and Nancy lose not only their money but also their ability to manage for themselves. By being robbed, they themselves become people who are wrong. And people who are wrong ought to be punished. Their quandary is that *they* were punished and thus became wrong, while the robbers who deprived them of their goods, of their pride, will not be convicted, will not lose their freedom—a prerogative of adults—and by the logic of getting what you deserve, end up vindicated while they, the victimized, stand convicted by their own loss.

The robbers were frightening people because they did not hesitate to use violence, or threats of violence, against other people, thus putting themselves in the same group as the Nazi exterminators of "Fainting on the Subway" and the bully of "The Baddest Girl in the Neighborhood". As Nancy says, therefore, it is a frightening world:

"It's terrible to be at the mercy of such people."

With such people at liberty, the virtuous are no longer safe, the defenseless—those without guns—are no longer safe, and no longer safe, are no longer virtuous, since one must take all necessary steps to save oneself. Otherwise, one has failed and one deserves what happens next. This is familiar reasoning. It is the reasoning which reacts to tragedy with shame; it is the reasoning which condemns the victims of the Holocaust; it is the reasoning which justifies the mounting arsenals; it is the reasoning which may bring about the end of the world. It is American reasoning which leads to an un–American conclusion. The end of an American story, as Hollywood knows and everyone knows, cannot be so somber. Pessimism, the "realism" of Europe, is pretentious in America. Hopelessness is ruled out because problems call for action, call for solution. "Don't just stand there, do something." and soon it will be clear that "Every cloud has a silver lining." "There's no place to go but up," after all.

4.7 ABSTRACTING OUT CULTURAL CONSTRUCTS

In the next chapter, these recurring, important cultural constructs which have been emerging from this discussion will be arranged into a grammar which attempts to formalize the relationships obtaining among them. Before going on to group the constructs, however, it is necessary to decide what should be considered a "construct" at all. In order to show how these culturally primitive notions were distilled from this very free-flowing, nonanalytic treatment of the stories, working through an analysis of an example sentence might well be more elucidating than an abstract methodological description.

Beginning with sentences taken from the analysis of the stories, such as this one from the discussion of "The Ordeal" (*Section* 4.5):

> Kate is truly worthy of respect since not only did she withstand the pain, want to know insistently and courageously, but she also responded positively to what might have been thought unpleasant news.

a transformation was made to re–organize the sentence syntactically into as simple a form as possible:

1. Kate should be respected because she withstood pain and wanted to "know" and responded positively to unpleasant news.

Those statements were then unpacked into simpler propositions:

2.
    a. Being respected is a good thing—people want to be respected.
    b. Some people are respected—there is some sort of important distinction being made between those who are respected and those who are not.
    c. People are respected who do certain types of things.
    d. "Withstanding pain," "wanting to know," "being courageous," and "responding positively to unpleasant news" are all examples of those things which deserve respect.

From elsewhere in the investigations (and by virtue of being a cultural initiate) I "know" that it is true that:

3.
    a. "Withstanding pain" is difficult and praiseworthy;
    b. "Wanting to know" is important;
    c. "Being courageous" is difficult and praiseworthy;

Therefore:

4. People who do things which are important, difficult, and praiseworthy are worthy of respect.

Given 2a ("Being respected is a good thing—people want to be respected") the following list of culturally significant propositions can be inferred:

5.

    a. People should withstand pain;
    b. People should want to know;
    c. People should be courageous;
    d. People should be able to "take it" well;
    e. People want to be respected.

Now, given that 5A ("People should withstand pain") is not an absolute statement about the world, but is a conditional statement, it is possible to continue the unpacking process further.

Presumably, some people do withstand pain and others do not, some people should be respected and others should not be. The distinction is more intuitive, less clear, than that distinguishing between something which IS and something which IS NOT, for example. People who DO what they SHOULD DO are people acting correctly, what we will call PROPER PEOPLE to distinguish them from the rest of humanity with whom they share the common features grouped under the heading PEOPLE. PROPER PEOPLE is, therefore, a special category of PEOPLE and, also, a special category of ADULTS. PROPER PEOPLE inherit all of the features of ADULTS because they are those PEOPLE who do what ADULTS KNOW they SHOULD DO.

These sorts of distinctions among categories of PEOPLE are extremely important for the members of the group which makes them.

For example, in many aspects of the American life, it matters legally if someone is a CHILD or an ADULT. We EXPECT different behavior from people of different sorts. They have different RIGHTS and NEEDS etc. and those items, RIGHTS and NEEDS, are <u>REAL</u>, they matter and we can debate exactly what is a RIGHT and what is a NEED and what is, somewhat less compelling, a WANT. Should a person be hungry and steal food because he does not work and has no money, the judgment of culpability is quite different depending on what class of person he is. A CHILD need not work, indeed cannot work, and should he be hungry someone else is at fault because some ADULT or ADULTS in the aggregate (SOCIETY) did not provide him with a basic human NEED (food). Should the culprit BE an ADULT who does not work, the issue is quite a bit more complex; a number of different constructs begin to come into play. If the ADULT does not work because there is no work, then he may or may not be guilty of being a very improper person (i.e. criminal). Every ADULT should be able to provide for his own NEEDS; failure to do so makes him less than a PROPER PERSON. However, if there is no work from him to do then there may be debate about his RESPONSIBILITY. Should he not work because he DOES NOT WANT to work, then he is clearly guilty because he is not DOING what an ADULT MUST DO.

Political arguments, disagreements of all sorts, struggles among the various interest groups in American Society revolve around these sorts of issues. We agree that there are NEEDS, RIGHTS, RESPONSIBILITIES, and given that "all men are created equal" and should have the RIGHT TO "equal opportunity," the question of what exactly is a RIGHT or a NEED arises constantly.

For example, is the opportunity for having sexual relations a PHYSICAL NEED or a PLEASURE? Prisoner Rights groups may argue that it is a NEED while Law and Order advocates may consider it a PLEASURE (i.e. a WANT). Being forced to concede that sex is pleasurable, a Rights Group may then insist that it is both a PLEASURE and a NEED and that, indeed, HUMAN BEINGS have a RIGHT to PLEASURE.

Not every American would agree with every one of those statements and not everyone will agree that the constructs on the List of Constructs are arranged correctly or that the lists are precisely the right set of constructs. However, this does not, in itself, diminish the validity of the lists. Most of us who consider ourselves to be American have something to say about each item on the Lists and about each statement in the previous short discussion or the extended discussion of classes of PERSON which follows the Lists themselves. Although we may not agree that "ADULTS MUST ACT in the face of DANGER," for example, some of us may see this statement as an absolute condition of ADULTHOOD and others believe it to be more accurately a SHOULD, however all of us would agree 1) some PEOPLE ARE ADULTS; 2) DOING/ACTING is something PEOPLE DO; 3) some things are DANGEROUS; 4) ADULTS MUST DO some things and 5) SHOULD DO other things. Thus these constructs have meaning, and the relations among the primitive elements which constitute them are worth thinking and talking about. We know that we are dealing with culturally salient material when we can dispute the boundary lines among categories and find it important to do so but agree that the primitive elements are real, important, and primary. Cross–culturally, the primitive elements may have similar names, but the relations among these elements might well be very very different without the common ground of agreement of members of the same culture.

Some time ago, I had a discussion with an Italian friend. We were talking about RIGHTS. He insisted that RIGHTS are given to the INDIVIDUAL by SOCIETY. SOCIETY NEEDS literate PEOPLE more than illiterate ones, for example, and therefore GRANTS the INDIVIDUAL the RIGHT to an EDUCATION.

I was somewhat dumbfounded by this argument even though I could not refute it. I certainly agree that an EDUCATED PERSON is more USEFUL to SOCIETY than one who cannot read or write. However, the argument seemed totally back-wards. The INDIVIDUAL, in my American scheme, HAS RIGHTS by virtue of being an INDIVIDUAL PERSON. SOCIETY consists somewhat amorphously of the government, other people, and everything importantly composed of a GROUP of PEOPLE of which the INDIVIDUAL is one. SOCIETY, such as it is, MUST RESPECT the RIGHTS of the INDIVIDUAL, but cannot GRANT RIGHTS TO the INDIVIDUAL.

The distinction is a crucial one. In one case, the Italian, SOCIETY is at the core of the WORLD and must be protected. It is also granted the role of actor much more than in the American scheme in which the INDIVIDUAL is actor at the center of the

WORLD and SOCIETY IS, as an American friend put it, "just a bunch of INDI-VIDUALS anyway." SOCIETY is not even found on our Lists because it seemed that everything which could be said about SOCIETY was somehow reducible to the relationship of one INDIVIDUAL to OTHER INDIVIDUALS. SOCIETY need not be mentioned specifically, as long as the INDIVIDUAL and his RELATIONSHIP with OTHER PEOPLE were both included. Seemingly, and this is the claim being made here, an Italian Grammar of Cultural Constructs would be very different from the American Grammar presented here.

5.

A GRAMMAR OF AMERICAN CULTURAL CONSTRUCTS

A compendium of cultural constructs could take the form of a simple list of statements which might read, for example:

1. ALL PEOPLE SHOULD BE HEALTHY
2. ALL PEOPLE DO NEED
3. ALL PEOPLE SHOULD BE HAPPY

Such a list would be convenient because each individual statement would be present in its full form, easy to read and to understand. However, a bit more structure seems necessary even for this simple three item list. Obviously, sentences (1) and (3) are more closely related to one another than they are to (3) since (1) and (3) have in common ALL PEOPLE SHOULD BE while (2) shares only ALL PEOPLE with them.

(1) (2) and (3) are all taken from this list below, in which all of the ALL PEOPLE SHOULD BE statements are grouped together, all of the ALL PEOPLE SHOULD NOT statements are grouped together, and so on.

(B.II.2) ALL PEOPLE SHOULD BE <u>ADULTS</u>.
      ALL PEOPLE SHOULD BE <u>HEALTHY</u>.
      ALL PEOPLE SHOULD BE <u>HAPPY</u>.
      ALL PEOPLE SHOULD BE <u>TRUSTWORTHY</u>.
      ALL PEOPLE SHOULD <u>WANT</u> what PEOPLE WANT.
(B.II.3) ALL PEOPLE <u>SHOULD NOT</u> HURT PEOPLE.
      ALL PEOPLE SHOULD NOT <u>Inhibit the FREEDOM of</u>

CHOICE OF OTHERS (except some members of their
FAMILY).
ALL PEOPLE SHOULD NOT Give in.
(B.II.4) ALL PEOPLE DO NEED.
ALL PEOPLE DO think.
ALL PEOPLE DO communicate, etc.
(B.II.5) ALL PEOPLE CAN ACT one way and BE another.
ALL PEOPLE CAN MANIPULATE OTHER PEOPLE.
ALL PEOPLE CAN BE BAD or GOOD
ALL PEOPLE CAN BE COMPETENT or INCOMPETENT.

(The numbers and letters in parenthesis (B.II.4) etc. indicate where these constructs
are to be found in the Grammar below.)

Clearly, the redundancy in these lists is enormous, written out in full, it is clear that

1. ALL PEOPLE CAN ACT one way and BE another
2. ALL PEOPLE CAN MANIPULATE OTHER PEOPLE
3. ALL PEOPLE CAN BE BAD OR GOOD
4. ALL PEOPLE CAN BE COMPETENT or INCOMPETENT

could be rewritten in an outline form as

ALL PEOPLE CAN
1. ACT one way and BE another
2. MANIPULATE OTHER PEOPLE
3. BE BAD or GOOD
4. COMPETENT or INCOMPETENT

In such a form, the more specific elements inherit the properties of the more general
predicate. Only those elements which undergo change are mentioned explicitly.
Higher level elements remain unchanged. These organized lists of statements are all
parts of a Psychology of HUMAN NATURE, one of the highest level structures of
the list (the others being THE NATURE OF THE WORLD [an Ontology] and
ADULTHOOD [which includes a section A PROPER PERSON, a Compendium of
Virtues]). Part of the subdivisions of this Psychology are as follows:

B. HUMAN NATURE
    II. ALL PEOPLE
        1. ARE
            EQUAL in RIGHTS and RESPONSIBILITIES

        ALIVE

        ALONE

        etc.

2. SHOULD

        BE

           ADULTS

           HEALTHY

           HAPPY

           TRUSTWORTHY

        WANT

        what PEOPLE WANT

3. SHOULD NOT

           HURT PEOPLE

           Inhibit FREEDOM OF CHOICE of

           OTHERS

           Give in

4. DO

        NEED

        think

        communicate

        etc.

Further specification is clearly possible.

In Chapter 6, many of these high level elements are drawn together into a "Story" detailing some of the types of persons existing in America. In this composite text, statements such as this appear:

CHILDREN HAVE FEELINGS, as do all PEOPLE, and if they DO NOT FEEL SAFE or FEEL HAPPY they ARE often unABLE to CONTROL their PAIN at UNSATISFIED NEEDS.

Exactly which NEEDS PEOPLE HAVE, for example are not spelled out. They are specified in the Grammar itself. In this case, the NEEDS an INDIVIDUAL HAS by virtue of BEING a PERSON can be found in Section B. (HUMAN NATURE), I (ALL PEOPLE), 1 (ARE) a (NEEDS).

In order to make the Grammar—as these structured lists are called—more accessible, a List of Lists is included. It contains only the higher level categories, showing their relationships to one another. The details can then be found on the List itself.

In the List of Lists, words or phrases in capital letters, for example FACTS, occur repeatedly in the Lists as more or less important primitive elements. Words or phrases in small letters are either words used to connect the Primitives ("for," "what") or items which do not occur repeatedly. Many of the capitalized words are found as primitive elements in Chapter 6, "AN AMERICAN STORY."

The List of Lists and the Grammar follow.

LIST OF LISTS

A. NATURE OF THE WORLD
  I. FACTS
    1. x EXISTS
    2. x DOES NOT EXIST
  II. y is POSSIBLE
  III. The physical world
  IV. LIFE IS
  V. REASONS why an "Organism" ACTS

B. HUMAN NATURE

  I. By virtue of being a PERSON, an INDIVIDUAL
    1. MUST
      a. CHOOSE
      b. EARN RIGHTS
      c. DO (SATISFY NEEDS)

    2. HAS
      a. NEEDS
          SOCIAL
          EMOTIONAL
          for SENSE OF SELF
          for FLEXIBILITY
          PHYSICAL
      b. FEELINGS
            ARE
      c. INALIENABLE RIGHTS
      d. PAIN occasionally

    3. MUST HAVE in order to DO
      a. KNOWLEDGE
      b. WORK
      c. FRIENDS
          ARE
          DO
          MUST BE
          CAN
          SHOULD BE

II. ALL PEOPLE (Inherit all properties of I.)
  1. ARE
     a. INDIVIDUALS (independent entity) (inherit
        all properties of I & II)
        —The INDIVIDUAL
        IS
        DOES
        MAY
        HAS
          SELF
          "TRUE SELF"
        (may) HAVE STRONG SELF

  2. SHOULD
          BE
          WANT
  3. SHOULD NOT
  4. DO
  5. CAN
  6. WANT
  7. DO NOT WANT

III. A PERSON MAY BE

  1. HAPPY
  2. COURAGEOUS
  3. STRONG
  4. RATIONAL
  5. RIGHT/WRONG

C. ADULTHOOD

  I. ADULTS
    1. ARE
    2. MUST
       a. BE
       b. DO
       c. HAVE

        d. BE ABLE TO

        e. KNOW

        f. WANT

        g. NEED

    3. SHOULD

        a. BE

        b. DO

        c. HAVE

    4. SHOULD NOT

II. A PROPER PERSON (inherits all ADULT properties)

    1. IS

    2. DOES

    3. HAS

    4. DOES NOT

    5. IS ABLE TO

THE GRAMMAR

A. NATURE OF THE WORLD

I. FACTS—Cultural entities or qualities whose existence is beyond dispute.

1. x EXISTS
   TRUTH
   CHANGE
   GROWTH
   CHOICE
   NEEDS
   PAIN
   RESPONSIBILITY
   RIGHTS
   GUILT
   HAPPINESS
   REALITY
   "REAL" WORLD
   FEELINGS
   "REAL FEELINGS"
   WHAT CAN BE KNOWN THROUGH THE SENSES
   UNDERSTANDING
   RESOURCES
   THE SELF
   THE "TRUE SELF"
   COURAGE
   STRENGTH
   FUN
   WORK
   HISTORY
   EQUALITY
   FRIENDS
   RELATIONSHIPS
   TIME
   PAST/PRESENT/FUTURE
   LOSS
   GAIN
   MONEY
   EXCHANGE

VALUE
SOCIETY
BEST INTEREST
KNOWING
DOING
EFFECTS OF ONE'S ACTIONS
RIGHT/WRONG
HOPE
THREATS
LIFE
INSANITY
BEING UNABLE TO STAND SOMETHING
INCOMPETENCE
FREEDOM
PREDICTION
COHERENCE
HEALTH/SICKNESS
FACTS
WINNING/LOSING
TRUST
SAFETY
DANGER
The INDIVIDUAL
PLEASURE
NECESSITIES
MITIGATING CIRCUMSTANCES
FAIRNESS
PROBLEMS
SOLUTIONS TO PROBLEMS
OTHER PEOPLE
THINGS PEOPLE CANNOT TOLERATE
                          CONTROL
          ARE NOT RESPONSIBLE FOR

2. THINGS THAT DO NOT EXIST
   ABSOLUTE SAFETY
   SOMEONE ELSE TO REALLY SATISFY ALL
     NEEDS
   STABILITY—Total PREDICTABILITY

II. Things that are possible but must be worked for

CHANGE for the better
"WINNING"
KNOWING the TRUTH
SOLVING PROBLEMS
"REAL" COMMUNICATION
CONSENSUS
CONTROL of SELF, OTHERS, ENVIRONMENT
MAKING A DECISION CORRECTLY
HAVING A MEANINGFUL EFFECT
HAVING A "REAL" CHOICE
BEING FREE
SATISFYING NEEDS
PREDICTING FUTURE WORLD

III. The physical world

IS ALWAYS CHANGING
IS ALL THAT "REALLY" EXISTS
CAN BE CONTROLLED (in part)
IS INDIFFERENT
IS UNSAFE (often)
CAN BE CHANGED (in large part)
IS complex
IS ALWAYS THE SAME
Imposes REAL constraints
is KNOWable

IV. LIFE IS

always CHANGING
always THE SAME
FAIR—"You get what you deserve"
NOT FAIR—"You don't always get what you deserve"
PRECIOUS
SHORT

V. REASONS an "Organism" ACTS

TO SURVIVE
TO SATISFY NEEDS

TO SOLVE PROBLEMS
TO GAIN COHERENCE
BECAUSE (action is) HEALTHY
                    USEFUL

B. HUMAN NATURE

   I. By virtue of BEING a PERSON, an INDIVIDUAL:
   1. MUST
     a. CHOOSE—Choice
          EXISTS
          IS A RESPONSIBILITY
          IS INESCAPABLE
     b. EARN RIGHTS—FULFILL RESPONSIBILITIES
     c. DO (SATISFY NEEDS)

   2. HAS
     a. NEEDS
       (SOCIAL)
          FRIENDS
          TIES
          SOMEONE TO TALK TO
       (EMOTIONAL)
          STABILITY
          SECURITY
          COHERENCE (WORLD SHOULD BE
            PREDICTABLE)
          To be LIKED
          TO FEEL
             HAPPY
             SATISFIED WITH SELF
      A SENSE OF SELF
      (FLEXIBILITY)
          LEARNING
          GROWING
          CHANGING
      (PHYSICAL)
          air
          space
          tolerable temperatures
          (some) money

                            privacy
                            cleanliness
                            sleep
                            water
                            SAFETY
                            FOOD
                                    is a PLEASURE
                                    "SAFE" topic of
                                        conversation
                                    may be very varied
                                    should be HEALTHY

  b. FEELINGS
     EXIST
     SHOULD BE TRUSTED MORE THAN BEHAVIOR
      (expressed) "REAL FEELINGS" are truer
      than BEHAVIOR)
     ARE
      JOY
      ANGER
      PAIN
      UNHAPPINESS
      LONELINESS
      SADNESS
      FREEDOM
      HAPPINESS
      STRENGTH
      VULNERABILITY
     (There are many more FEELINGS)
     MAY GET "OUT OF CONTROL"
     INFLUENCE BEHAVIOR
     PROPER RESPONSES
     SHOULD BE ACKNOWLEDGED
     MAY INFLUENCE RESPONSIBILITY FOR ACTION
     MAY BE APPROPRIATE OR NOT
  c. INALIENABLE RIGHTS
     TO HAVE PHYSICAL NEEDS SATISFIED
     TO LIVE
     TO HAVE CHOICES (exactly which ones
      depend on circumstances)
     TO BE HAPPY
     TO BE HEALTHY

TO TRUST THAT THE WORLD MAKES SENSE
TO HAVE (some) POSSESSIONS

d. PAIN

EXISTS
HURTS
CAN BE PHYSICAL or MENTAL
CAN BE WITHSTOOD
VARIES in intensity
IS UPSETTING
MAY BE AN EXCUSE for not fulfilling
   RESPONSIBILITY
MAY BE NECESSARY
              GROWTH
              CHANGE require some pain
IS the RESULT of DOING WRONG
IS the RESULT of CHOOSING INCORRECTLY
CAN EXPIATE FOR WRONGDOING
CAUSES other PEOPLE to WANT to HELP
PHYSICAL PAIN RESULTS FROM
              DEPRIVATION OF PHYSICAL NEED
              DISEASE
              LACK OF SAFETY
MENTAL PAIN
              RESULTS FROM DEPRIVATION
              OF EMOTIONAL NEED
              MAY BE self-generated

3. MUST HAVE in order to DO

a. KNOWLEDGE

EXISTS
PERMITS CONTROL over the WORLD
ALLOWS FOR SOLVING OF PROBLEMS
GIVES POWER to the possessor
MAKES WORLD MAKE SENSE:
              Permits PLANNING
              Increases FEELING OF
              SAFETY

b. WORK

EXISTS
MUST BE DONE
IS NOT FUN

IS IMPORTANT
Pays—PERMITS PERSON to buy (SATISFY)
    NEEDS
    PLEASURES
c. FRIENDS
 ARE
  USEFUL
  GOOD for the HEALTH
  PEOPLE who like each other
  CHOSEN
  similar
  different
  there when they are needed
  HONEST with each other
  demanding
  someone a PERSON can be
   GENUINELY himself with
 DO
  take PLEASURE in their
   RELATIONSHIP
  RESPECT each other
  share experiences—talk to
   each other
  take each other's parts in
   arguments
  INVEST TIME in each other
 MUST BE
  EQUALS
  HAPPY in the RELATIONSHIP
 CAN
  HURT each other for the
   other's BENEFIT
  SATISFY NEEDS
     SOCIAL NEEDS (overcome
      loneliness)
  BE outgrown
  HELP
  FEEL good about SELF
  TEACH
  GUIDE
  CHALLENGE
  SHOULD BE CHANGED when no longer useful

II. ALL PEOPLE

  1. ARE
           EQUAL in RIGHTS and RESPONSIBILITIES
           ALIVE
           ALONE
           Upset by PAIN
           VULNERABLE—can be hurt
           MORTAL
           PART OF SOCIETY
           INDIVIDUALS (Independent Entities)
    a. The INDIVIDUAL
      IS
        OF PRIMARY IMPORTANCE
        ALONE in the WORLD
        most important to SELF
      DOES
        CHOOSE his LIFE
        CREATE his LIFE
        CONTROL his fate
      MAY
        CHANGE the WORLD
      HAS
        INALIENABLE RIGHTS
        NEEDS
        personal history
        FUTURE
        (some) PERSONAL POWER
        "TRUE SELF"
            EXISTS (in an EMOTIONAL WORLD)
            FEELS
            EXPERIENCES
            reacts to stimuli
            surfaces in times of stress
            CAN BE KNOWN
            IS who a PERSON REALLY IS
        SELF which
            CHANGES as a RESULT of
                CHOICES
                ACTIONS
                EXPERIENCE (LEARNING)
                TIME

EXISTS in the PHYSICAL and
SOCIAL WORLD
IS the "DOER" which the WORLD
assumes "IS" the PERSON
(may) HAVE
STRONG SELF
DOES (satisfies NEEDS)
Only "REAL" NECESSITY of ADULTS
MUST
Rely only on SELF to DO (satisfy NEEDS)

2. SHOULD
BE
ADULTS
HEALTHY
HAPPY
TRUSTWORTHY
WANT what PEOPLE WANT

3. SHOULD NOT
HURT PEOPLE
Inhibit FREEDOM or CHOICE of OTHERS
(except FAMILY)
Give in

4. DO
NEED
think
communicate
eat
breathe
FEEL
eliminate
WANT
react
*CHANGE
*CHOOSE
*KNOW
*DO (SATISFY NEEDS)
*PLAN
*PREDICT   *classes of persons differ
on these qualities (see List of Lists)

5. CAN
   ACT one way and BE another
   MANIPULATE OTHER PEOPLE
   Be BAD or GOOD
      COMPETENT or INCOMPETENT
      COURAGEOUS or COWARDLY etc.
   CHANGE
   BE FOOLED
   KNOW THE TRUTH

6. WANT
   TO BE
      SECURE
      ADULTS
      NORMAL
      HAPPY
      HEALTHY
      INDEPENDENT
      FREE
      Not tied down

7. DO NOT WANT
            UNHAPPINESS
            UNPLEASANTNESS
            PAIN

III. A PERSON MAY BE

1. HAPPY (opposite: UNHAPPY)
            NORMAL STATE OF PEOPLE
      signals NEEDS are SATISFIED

2. COURAGEOUS (opposite: COWARDLY)
            CAN withstand PAIN
            WANTS to KNOW (bad news)
      resists oppression

3. STRONG (opposite: WEAK)
            HELP weak
            CAN SATISFY NEEDS
      not very VULNERABLE

not easily THREATENED
not AFRAID of being HURT

4. RATIONAL (opposite: IRRATIONAL)
   CAN UNDERSTAND
   USES MIND to SOLVE PROBLEMS
   CAN CONTROL FEELINGS
   CAN MAKE DECISIONS
         PLAN
         CHOOSE

5. RIGHT (opposite: WRONG)
       KNOW the TRUTH (one meaning)
       BEHAVE CORRECTLY (second meaning)

C. CLASSES OF PERSONS (all classes inherit properties of all PEOPLE)

   I. ADULTS

      1. ARE PEOPLE who
          SATISFY NEEDS for themSELVES
          CAN DO what they SHOULD and MUST DO
           to SURVIVE
          WORK
          KNOW what they MUST KNOW in order to DO

      2. MUST
        a. BE
          RESPONSIBLE for SELF
        b. DO
          Protect themSELVES
          SATISFY (own) NEEDS
          CHOOSE
          DECIDE
          Distinguish between REALITY and
           ILLUSION
          ACT as if ALONE
          WORK
          SOLVE PROBLEMS
          ACT in the face of DANGER
          PREDICT

```
        PLAN
c.  HAVE
        FUTURE (hope)
        SENSE OF SELF

d.  BE ABLE to
        SOLVE PROBLEMS
        CHOOSE PROPERLY
        ACT EFFECTIVELY on CHOICES
        CHANGE
        WITHSTAND what is BEARABLE
        MANAGE THEIR LIVES
        SURVIVE
        KNOW

e.  KNOW
        what EXISTS
        what DOES NOT EXIST
        what IS POSSIBLE
        about HUMAN NATURE
        how the WORLD IS
        what IS a PROBLEM
        what CAN BE DONE
        what CAN NOT BE DONE
        how to PROTECT themSELVES
        how to SOLVE PROBLEMS
        how to SATISFY NEEDS
        DISTINGUISH between
                TRUTH and FALSEHOOD
                REALITY and ILLUSION
                NEEDS and WANTS
        that things ARE NOT what they SEEM
    whom to TRUST
    what are PROPER GROUNDS for a DECISION
    what can be TOLERATED
    things can be in their BEST INTEREST
        if they ARE:
        ECONOMICALLY ADVANTAGEOUS
        EMOTIONALLY ADVANTAGEOUS
            (makes them FEEL HAPPY
                        GOOD
                        STRONG
                        SAFE)
```

HEALTHY
IN OTHER PEOPLE'S BEST INTEREST
(BEING HELPFUL   (SATISFYING NEED)
CARING
MAKES HELPER
FEEL GOOD
CARING
HELPFUL
STRONG
SAFE)

f. WANT
TO BE HAPPY
TO BE RESPECTED
TO BE SAFE
TO BE HEALTHY
TO BE LOVED
TO BE LIKED
TO HAVE PLEASURES

g. NEED IN ORDER TO BE PROPER PERSONS
TO KNOW
TO BE ABLE TO DO
TO DO
TO HAVE CHOICES
THE WORLD TO BE COHERENT
ONLY THEMSELVES

3. SHOULD
a. BE
RATIONAL
STRONG
INDEPENDENT (SATISFY own NEEDS)
HAPPY
COURAGEOUS
RESPONSIBLE
for OTHERS
for ACTIONS
REALISTIC
FREE
dependable
flexible

       effective

       co-operative

       COMPETENT (DO things well)

       RATIONAL

       FRIENDLY

       HELPFUL

       TRUSTWORTHY (WILL BE and ACT like
          ADULTS ARE and ACT)

       focused on the FUTURE

b. DO

       ACT in own BEST INTEREST

       DECIDE PROPERLY (in own BEST INTEREST)

       CHOOSE CORRECTLY

          for SELF

          to BE, DO, ACT like ADULT

       MAKE FRIENDS

       TRUST themSELVES

       LOVE themSELVES

       LIKE themSELVES

         OTHER PEOPLE

       ACCEPT REALITY (strength and constraints)

       CHANGE

       HELP others (SATISFY NEEDS)

       ACT rather than not ACT

       LET GO of what is not good for SELF

c. HAVE

       FRIENDS

       RELATIONSHIPS

       FUN

       JOB

       MONEY

4. SHOULD NOT

       NEED OTHER PEOPLE

       dwell on the past

       make a fuss

       leave loose ends

       TAKE RESPONSIBILITY for PEOPLE who SHOULD
          SATISFY OWN NEEDS

II. PROPER PERSON (inherits all of ADULT properties)

IS
    WHAT ADULT IS and SHOULD BE
DOES

    WHAT ADULT DOES and CAN BE
HAS

    WHAT ADULT NEEDS and WANTS

DOES NOT SUFFER

IS ABLE TO
    HELP OTHERS
    DECIDE for OTHERS (who CANNOT DECIDE)

6.

AN AMERICAN STORY[1,2]

ADULTS are INDIVIDUAL PEOPLE WHO KNOW HOW to DO what they MUST DO; CAN DO what they MUST DO; and DO it. They UNDERSTAND that "There are two profound choices in life: to accept things as they exist or to accept the responsibility for changing them" (Koberg & Bagnall, 1976 p. 41). They HAVE the CHOICE they HAVE the KNOWLEDGE and they CHANGE and DO to SATISFY their NEEDS. They HAVE the RESPONSIBILITY for DOing and the RIGHT to CHOOSE what and how they should live their lives, manage their affairs, and SATISFY their NEEDS. Their NEEDS SATISFIED, they FEEL GOOD about themselves and HAVE EARNED the RIGHT to PLEASURE and HAPPINESS.

ADULTS KNOW what they SHOULD BE, what they SHOULD DO, what they SHOULD HAVE. They KNOW what is "worth bothering with." They live in the PRESENT but DECIDE what is IN THEIR BEST INTEREST for the FUTURE. They KNOW HOW THE WORLD IS, WHAT is POSSIBLE, and they USE PAST

---

[1]In this text, as in the Lists, some words are in upper case and others in lower case. NEEDS, for example, is capitalized, while "they," "try," "instead of," "ice cream," and "mental hospital" are in small letters. The capitalized words are almost all words which appear importantly on the Lists: the uncapitalized words are of three types: (1) "connecting" words: prepositions, pronouns, conjunctions, etc. These grammatical words communicate a set of possible relationships which may well be culturally determined since they express what is, and how what is interacts with other things which also are; (2) words such as "small," "return," or "promise" which do not add very much to the discussion but help clarify a point which is being made; (3) words such as "ice cream" or "mental hospital" which conjure up a whole world. The associations and richness of these words lends some power to our description. There are some words, "upset" is one, which felt clearly like a #2 uncapitalized word as we began our Story and then was so important to the discussion that it "grew" into a capitalized primitive.

[2]As should be clear to all readers of this book, "An American Story" is not really a story at all since it lacks both Events and Evaluation. Rather, the Story is a grammar of possible stories. Each sentence should be read as a compressed form of a myriad of "real" stories of the sort looked at earlier and the whole text composed of these sentences results in this most general level of Story: the generic American Story.

EXPERIENCE (what WAS in the PAST) to help them PLAN what to DO in the FUTURE. They KNOW that the WORLD is NOT PREDICTABLE, that they are not ABSOLUTELY SAFE because they DO NOT KNOW what will happen in the FUTURE and NOT to KNOW is very UNSAFE. When a PERSON DOES NOT KNOW, the WORLD BECOMES INCOHERENT and the INDIVIDUAL might not BE ABLE TO STAND it and DIE (HAVE NO FUTURE) or GO CRAZY— become one who DOES NOT KNOW, CANNOT DO and is less than an ADULT.

An ADULT MUST KNOW and MUST BE ABLE to TAKE IT, to WITH-STAND PAIN, to KNOW that he HAS a FUTURE and that the FUTURE is BETTER THAN THE PAST. KNOWing about the WORLD allows the PERSON to PLAN and if he PLANS CORRECTLY (CHOOSES what to DO REAL-ISTICALLY), he will HAVE what he WANTS and BE ABLE to SATISFY his own NEEDS. If he does not PLAN CORRECTLY, UNDERSTAND what an ADULT MUST, then he will NOT HAVE what he WANTS and may not BE ABLE to SATISFY his own NEEDS. Therefore, NOT HAVING is proof of the FACT of NOT BEING an ADULT since an ADULT HAS what he NEEDS and CAN DO what he MUST DO in order to SATISFY those NEEDS.

EVERY INDIVIDUAL PERSON WANTS to be an ADULT, TO BE INDE-PENDENT, to NEED only himSELF to SATISFY his NEEDS. The TRUTH of the WORLD is that each INDIVIDUAL IS ALONE and MUST SATISFY his own NEEDS because he CANNOT DEPEND on anOTHER PERSON to SATISFY his NEEDS in all circumstances. An INDIVIDUAL CAN HOPE that anOTHER will ALWAYS HELP, but it IS NOT TRUE that this is the case. In order to BE SAFE, to KNOW that NEEDS will be SATISFIED, EVERY PERSON WANTS to NEED only himSELF, because EVERY INDIVIDUAL *HAS* A SELF, just as he HAS a BODY and IS ALIVE. He *HAS* it and he HAS a FUTURE until he DIES when he no longer HAS NEEDS—for AIR, WATER, SLEEP, FOOD—or WANTS, no longer EATS, BREATHES, SLEEPS, DRINKS, ELIMINATES, or LIVES. If his SELF CAN SATISFY his NEEDS he is SAFE because he WILL HAVE a SELF until he HAS NO MORE NEEDS.

As long as he LIVES, the INDIVIDUAL MUST SOLVE PROBLEMS. THINK-ING, SPEAKING, ACTING, PLANNING—the INDIVIDUAL USES what he KNOWS to SATISFY his own NEEDS and the NEEDS and WANTS of OTHERS, FAMILY, and FRIENDS. When there is DANGER, the ADULT ACTS to PRO-TECT himSELF to avoid PAIN and SUFFERING. If anOTHER PERSON SUF-FERS PAIN, the ADULT MUST HELP the OTHER FEEL BETTER because PAIN and UNHAPPINESS are PROBLEMS which MUST BE SOLVED. SOLV-ING PROBLEMS, SATISFYING NEEDS, and OBTAINING WANTS ARE the activities of an ADULT.

PEOPLE who DO NOT KNOW and CANNOT KNOW are not ADULTS, therefore, a PROBLEM without a SOLUTION which the INDIVIDUAL CAN DISCOVER makes him LESS, something other, than a full PERSON. It IS THREATENING to an INDIVIDUAL to find a PROBLEM which he CANNOT SOLVE, a PERSON who CANNOT BE HELPED or MADE HAPPY, because such a situation makes the INDIVIDUAL UNDERSTAND that HE CANNOT DO, CANNOT KNOW and therefore is NOT SAFE. If he CANNOT DO what an ADULT MUST DO then he CANNOT TRUST himSELF to TAKE CARE of his own NEEDS and he IS, indeed, ALONE, HELPLESS, and VULNERABLE like a CHILD and unlike an ADULT.

CHILDREN CANNOT DO, DO NOT KNOW. They LEARN and CHANGE and BECOME ADULTS through TIME. As long as they are small, however, they HAVE SPECIAL NEEDS. They MUST BE CARED FOR, HELPED, LOVED, and HAVE their NEEDS SATISFIED by OTHERS who LOVE them. CHILDREN HAVE a FUTURE. They HAVE the capacity to BECOME ADULTS and MUST be TAUGHT by ADULTS what the WORLD is like. CHILDREN DO NOT KNOW and therefore CANNOT CHOOSE how to LIVE LIFE. It is important that CHIL-DREN HAVE their HUMAN NEEDS and SPECIAL NEEDS satisfied because they are CHANGING as the RESULT of their EXPERIENCES of the WORLD and of OTHER PEOPLE. PEOPLE MUST HAVE a HAPPY PAST in order to TRUST the WORLD enough to BECOME PROPER PEOPLE and DO what they SHOULD DO. CHILDREN HAVE a developing SELF with its own DEVELOP-ING SELF—INTEREST. If a CHILD IS to UNDERSTAND that HE SHOULD BE GOOD and LIVE HAPPILY with OTHER PEOPLE, he MUST UNDER-STAND that it IS in his BEST INTEREST to DO SO. The best way to show a CHILD that his BEST INTEREST lies in WORKING to SATISFY his OWN NEEDS is for the CHILD to have a CHILDHOOD which is PLEASANT enough so that he BELIEVES the WORLD to BE COHERENT and that he CAN PLAN and PREDICT and ACT to GET what HE WANTS. If a CHILD'S NEEDS went UNSATISFIED, he MIGHT LEARN that the WORLD WAS NOT a SAFE PLACE or a PREDICTABLE one and therefore he SHOULD either DO NOTH-ING (to PROTECT himSELF) or ACT WRONGLY (in order to GET what he NEEDed and WANTed in any way that WAS POSSIBLE.)

CHILDREN HAVE FEELINGS, as do all PEOPLE, and if they DO NOT FEEL SAFE or FEEL HAPPY they ARE often unABLE to CONTROL their PAIN at UNSATISFIED NEEDS. They may be FRIGHTENED, for example, at something which an ADULT would KNOW would not HURT them. CHILDREN are LEARNING how to PREDICT, HOW to PLAN, how to CONTROL their environ-ment, their FEELINGS, and ultimately themSELVES.

CHILDREN MUST be TAKEN CARE OF, but they are not FRIGHTENING or UPSETTING to OTHER PEOPLE. Although they ARE NOT TRUSTWORTHY because they ARE NOT ABLE to CONTROL their EMOTIONS and UNDER-STAND the meaning of their ACTIONS, CHILDREN are small enough physically NOT to THREATEN OTHER PEOPLE'S HEALTH—they are not STRONG enough to HURT someone else. Since they HAVE a FUTURE, even more than a PRESENT or a PAST, they MAKE OTHER PEOPLE HAPPY. They will GROW and BECOME ADULTS. It is not their role to be DEPENDENT and "a burden" to OTHERS until they DIE.

CHILDREN HAVE NEEDS and PROBLEMS, but an ADULT CAN HELP a

CHILD and assure him that the PAIN WILL NOT LAST FOREVER and that in the FUTURE he will be HAPPY and FREE of PAIN. HELPING a CHILD is USEFUL—it IS NOT "wasted effort." CHILDREN WILL BE ABLE to SATISFY their OWN NEEDS someday and they PAY for their PRESENT HELPLESSNESS with the promise of FUTURE ADULTHOOD.

CHILDREN ARE NOT ADULTS, but unlike ALL OTHER PEOPLE who DO NOT BEHAVE like ADULTS, they bring JOY to OTHER PEOPLE and represent the FUTURE. Therefore they ARE LOVED and CARED FOR while the SICK, the MORIBUND, and the RETARDED are alternatively PITIED and DESPISED; the CRAZY are PITIED and FEARED; and the POOR and the CRIMINAL are FEAR-ED and HATED and sometimes PITIED. EACH INDIVIDUAL HAS NEEDS and HAS A RIGHT for those NEEDS to be SATISFIED. All of those PEOPLE MUST BE TAKEN CARE OF but very few INDIVIDUALS of those groups of PEOPLE WILL ever BECOME an ADULT, LIVE PROPERLY, HAVE A FUTURE, and stop MAKING OTHER PEOPLE UNHAPPY.

The SICK may BECOME WELL. In that case, they return to their own LIVES and begin once again to SATISFY their own NEEDS. They HAVE a FUTURE and therefore can be TRUSTED to BEHAVE CORRECTLY since it is NOT in the BEST INTEREST of the INDIVIDUAL to DO anything which would MAKE him LESS HAPPY or SAFE in the FUTURE. The MORIBUND are LESS TRUST-WORTHY. They HAVE "nothing to lose." Lacking a FUTURE, they lack a BEST INTEREST and also any reason to PLAN out their ACTIONS to MAKE themselves HAPPY. They ARE DYING. They HAVE no reason to BE HAPPY. They MAKE the LIVING uncomfortable since it is PAINFUL to watch someone in TROUBLE and BE UNABLE to HELP. HELPLESSNESS in the face of a PROBLEM renders the would be HELPER HELPLESS, thus reducing him from an ADULT to a CHILD. The SICK and the MORIBUND DESERVE some of their PAIN because they make OTHER PEOPLE SUFFER through BEING UNABLE to HELP.

CAUSING PAIN is WRONG and WRONGDOING SHOULD BE PUNISHED by PAIN. PAIN is also cleansing; it relieves the GUILT of WRONGDOING. Since the SICK PAID for their WRONGDOING by SUFFERING while they were ILL, the "score is even" and without onus they re-enter their LIVES HEALTHY and ABLE to SATISFY their OWN NEEDS. The MORIBUND DIE, of course, and their score is settled, too. They SUFFERED and MADE OTHERS SUFFER, but they "paid their debts" by dying and can BE thought of by the LIVING in terms of their LIFE as an ADULT before becoming MORIBUND and their BEHAVIOR during the time when it was clear that they HAD NO FUTURE. Since DYING is INTOLERABLE someone who managed to STAND what CANNOT BE STOOD and BE COURAGEOUS in the face of terrible PAIN and LOSS, may be closer in his DEATH to being a PROPER PERSON than he ever was in LIFE.

The SICK and the MORIBUND are ADULTS manqué: they KNOW what ADULTS NEED to KNOW but they CANNOT DO. The RETARDED DO NOT KNOW and CANNOT DO. They are CHILDREN without a FUTURE: CHIL-

DREN manqué. As CHILDREN they DESERVE to HAVE their NEEDS TAKEN CARE OF including the SPECIAL NEEDS of CHILDHOOD: LOVE, FUN, TO BE TAUGHT. But because they are LESS than CHILDREN, their NEEDS ARE TAKEN CARE OF at a lower level. They NEED FUN, for example, but not every day; they SHOULD HAVE SPECIAL FOODS, ice cream, perhaps, but only occasionally. Because they will NEVER BE ABLE to REPAY what they ARE GIVEN, they ARE GIVEN less—only enough to SATISFY the NEED for it HAVING BEEN GIVEN, but not so much that OTHERS with MORE FUTURE will be deprived.

The RETARDED in many hospitals are ranked according to how well they CAN THINK, how close to BEING an ADULT they can possibly BECOME. Those with the most capacity for KNOWING HAVE MORE NEEDS because they KNOW about their NEEDS and ARE MORE UPSET by those NEEDS BEING UN-SATISFIED. In mental hospitals for the CRAZY there is the same system of ranking by distance from the ADULT. The CRAZY MAY or MAY NOT KNOW, MAY or MAY NOT BE ABLE TO DO. They ARE CONFUSED and they ARE CONFUS-ING. They ARE CONFUSING because they ARE CONFUSED. Their WORLD is NOT COHERENT; it MAKES NO SENSE and PEOPLE CANNOT TOLERATE the WORLD BEING INCOHERENT. They HAVE NO CHOICE in an IN-COHERENT WORLD but to GO CRAZY because they are UNABLE to PLAN or PREDICT, to FEEL SAFE or SECURE, which ARE HUMAN NEEDS. Therefore, the CRAZY PERSON HAS NO CHOICE but to remain CRAZY—NOT TO CHANGE. Someone who DOES NOT CHANGE to HELP STOP his own PAIN is CONFUSING because PEOPLE SHOULD DO that and SHOULD WANT to STOP their PAIN but CRAZY PEOPLE MAY KNOW what PEOPLE WANT and MAY WANT what PEOPLE WANT but because they KNOW that the WORLD is INCOHERENT they CANNOT ACT to CHANGE. Since they CANNOT ACT TO CHANGE, they have no CHOICE but to remain CRAZY and therefore they HAVE NO FUTURE, they CAN NEVER CHANGE.

Sometimes it MAY SEEM as if a CRAZY PERSON has CHANGED and BE-COME UNCRAZY, NORMAL, ADULT. But that IS an ILLUSION because RE-ALLY in their TRUE SELVES they ARE PEOPLE who KNOW differently from OTHER PEOPLE and CANNOT BE TRUSTED. PEOPLE DO NOT KNOW what a CRAZY PERSON thinks is in his BEST INTEREST, someone who is so CONFUSED that he THINKS the WORLD is INCOHERENT and CANNOT STAND IT MAY DECIDE that his BEST INTEREST is different from what OTHER PEOPLE KNOW their BEST INTEREST to BE. Therefore, a CRAZY PERSON MAY BE UNPREDICTABLE and MAKE OTHERS FEEL UNSAFE because they WILL NOT KNOW what to EXPECT and PEOPLE NEED TO KNOW what to EXPECT if they ARE to FEEL SAFE. CRAZY PEOPLE are DIFFERENT PEOPLE, CONFUSING PEOPLE. ARE they ADULTS? No. ARE they CHILDREN? No. They KNOW and they CAN DO. They are DIFFERENT because they are CONFUSED and they ARE CONFUSING because they ARE DIFFERENT. But they ARE in PAIN and they CAUSE OTHER PEOPLE PAIN

by their PAIN and their CONFUSION. Therefore, their SUFFERING is DE-
SERVED. OTHER PEOPLE may PITY them but also DESPISE them for BEING
WRONG, KNOWING something which is not TRUE, KNOWing an ILLUSION
to BE REAL. CRAZY PEOPLE KNOW that PEOPLE NEED TIES, FRIENDS,
FAMILY, and a place in a COMMUNITY. They KNOW, too, that they ARE NOT
TRUSTED and DO NOT HAVE those TIES because they ARE DIFFERENT from
OTHER PEOPLE. They KNOW their NEEDS ARE NOT BEING SATISFIED
and they FEEL the PAIN of that deprivation. They KNOW they ARE ALONE
both as EVERY INDIVIDUAL IS ALONE and even more ALONE because they
DO NOT HAVE what OTHER PEOPLE HAVE to HELP them FEEL LESS
ALONE even if they ARE ALONE.

The CRAZY are CONFUSING because their PAIN is a PROBLEM which they
CANNOT SOLVE and which no OTHER PERSON CAN SOLVE either. Their
PAIN is almost a CHOICE because they SEEM not to WANT to KNOW or to
ACCEPT what OTHER PEOPLE KNOW:

There are THINGS which NO ONE CAN STAND and, yet, NOT STANDING
SOMETHING which NO ONE CAN STAND IS WRONG because probably the
INDIVIDUAL COULD HAVE CHOSEN to STAND IT. However, if a PERSON
DID NOT STAND SOMETHING and WAS in PAIN from it, *and* if the PERSON
was a PROPER PERSON otherwise and KNEW himSELF to BE WRONG, SICK
AND KNOWing things which ARE NOT REAL, then perhaps that PERSON
WAS only a SICK ADULT and NOT A CRAZY PERSON and CAN BE restored
to BEING an ADULT.

CRAZY PEOPLE ARE NOT RESPONSIBLE for their ACTIONS, unlike
ADULTS, because they DO NOT KNOW that they ARE DOING WRONG. They
may THINK (WRONGLY) that they are SATISFYING A NEED by DOING
something WRONG, something which CAUSES PAIN or LOSS to OTHER PEO-
PLE. CRIMINALS ARE ADULTS. They ARE WRONG ADULTS and they ARE
RESPONSIBLE for their ACTIONS. CRIMINALS ARE ADULTS who KNOW
what ADULTS KNOW, CAN DO what ADULTS CAN DO and yet CHOOSE to
DO as ADULTS KNOW they SHOULD NOT DO.

ADULTS KNOW that they MUST NOT KILL, or TAKE what someone else
OWNS, or cause PAIN to ANY OTHER PERSON *except* in the BEST INTEREST
of that PERSON. CRIMINALS KNOW all that and yet they CHOOSE to DO
WRONG. They MUST BE PUNISHED. Because they CHOOSE WRONGLY,
they MUST BE DEPRIVED of CHOICE: because they are ADULTS who CHOSE
NOT TO ACT RESPONSIBLY, like ADULTS—they MUST BE TREATED
LIKE CHILDREN who NEED TO BE PUNISHED "for their own good," deprived
of FREEDOM, of PLEASURE, of CONTROL OVER THEIR OWN LIVES.
Unlike CHILDREN, they ARE NOT LOVED or considered to HAVE SPECIAL
NEEDS. They ARE ADULTS and their NEEDS are the NEEDS of an ADULT, not
the NEEDS of a CHILD which are only WANTS of an ADULT. Only the PHYS-
ICAL NEEDS of criminals MUST BE SATISFIED: to EAT, to DRINK, to BE

CLEAN; SOCIAL and SPIRITUAL NEEDS are left UNSATISFIED. The PAIN of UNSATISFIED NEEDS and the possibility of a FUTURE of UNSATISFIED NEEDS PAY BACK the WRONGNESS of the CRIMINAL ACT and, at the same time, TEACH the CRIMINAL that he MUST CHOOSE CORRECTLY when he HAS DECISIONS to MAKE in the FUTURE. DEPRIVING the CRIMINAL of a part of his FUTURE, of CONTROL over a part of his LIFE, is one part of the PAIN of imprisonment. He MUST PAY BACK his "debt to society" with HIS TIME, his FUTURE, his LIFE.

CRIMINALS MUST LEARN that WORK, which is UNPLEASANT and TIME CONSUMING for EVERYONE MUST NOT BE AVOIDED. "Getting something for nothing" IS IMPOSSIBLE since, if NO ONE WORKED—and NO ONE WANTS to WORK—NO ONE's NEEDS WOULD BE SATISFIED. WORK is NECESSARY both for the INDIVIDUAL to SATISFY his NEEDS and for SOCI-ETY, the GROUP of ALL INDIVIDUALS, to SATISFY its NEEDS. NOT WORKing HURTS EVERYONE because ALL MUST WORK if LIFE IS to CON-TINUE. CRIMINALS ARE, therefore, GUILTY of NOT WORKing as well as of the crime which they committed. The POOR ARE GUILTY only of NOT WORK-ing—of HAVING NEEDS and insufficient MEANS to SATISFY them.

The POOR KNOW that WORK is NECESSARY. They ARE POOR BECAUSE THEY ARE NOT WORKing, NOT WORKing enough, or NOT ABLE to WORK, depending on the circumstances. They KNOW that ADULTS WORK and often they MAY WANT to WORK but they ARE UNABLE to SATISFY their NEED to HAVE WORK in order to MAKE ENOUGH MONEY to SATISFY their OTHER NEEDS. Since ADULTS HAVE (some) MONEY, enough for their NEEDS, and DO WORK, the POOR ARE NOT ADULTS. If they DO WORK, they DO NOT WORK well because if they WORKED well they would be paid enough to SATISFY their NEEDS. This is only FAIR, only RATIONAL. Since they DO NOT HAVE they MUST NOT WANT or are UNABLE to WORK; in either case, the POOR ARE PEOPLE manqué—they DO NOT HAVE what they NEED and CANNOT DO what they MUST DO in order to SATISFY them.

The POOR may BE GOOD—they MAY WANT to WORK and to DO what PEOPLE SHOULD DO in order to BE what PEOPLE SHOULD BE, but they CANNOT and their NEEDS MUST BE TAKEN CARE OF by OTHER PEOPLE since it IS WRONG to allow any PERSON to STARVE or DIE of the COLD. They CANNOT PAY in MONEY and, unlike the CRIMINAL, they HAVE NOT CHOSEN to ACT INCORRECTLY, so they CANNOT BE DENIED their FREE-DOM of MOVEMENT and DECISION. But they ARE WRONG because they ARE NOT ADULTS who PROVIDE for themSELVES. They ARE also UN-TRUSTWORTHY since their LIVES MAY BE so UNHAPPY because of what they DO NOT HAVE and therefore CANNOT DO that they WILL DO something which is not ordinarily in the BEST INTEREST of the INDIVIDUALS in SOCIETY who DO HAVE. They MAY LET their FEELINGS GET OUT OF CONTROL and become CRAZY or CRIMINAL—reacting to the UNBEARABLE by MAK-

ING the WORLD UNSAFE for OTHERS. If they "have nothing to lose," they may well try to TAKE what IS not theirs instead of WORKING to BUY what they WANT like ADULTS and especially PROPER PEOPLE ARE ABLE to DO.

PROPER PEOPLE ARE those who DO what ADULTS SHOULD DO; who ARE what ADULTS should BE and who HAVE what ADULTS SHOULD HAVE. Since PEOPLE CANNOT KNOW what OTHER PEOPLE "TRULY ARE" or exactly what they "ACTUALLY DO," they assume AN INDIVIDUAL is a PROPER PERSON If he HAS what PEOPLE WANT TO HAVE: MONEY, FAMILY, FRIENDS, a good JOB, POWER, RESPECT. Someone who HAS all that he NEEDS and WANTS *IS* TRUSTWORTHY because he KNOWS HOW to SATIS-FY his NEEDS and his KNOWing is PROVED by his NEEDS being SATISFIED. Since he is NOT a CRIMINAL, he MUST KNOW better than OTHER PEOPLE because he WANTS and CAN GET what he WANTS and they CANNOT. He has no NEED or DESIRE to MAKE DECISIONS other than those which have EN-ABLED him to GET what he HAS, and since he IS who he IS and HAS what he HAS, he MUST BE someone who CAN CONTROL the WORLD sufficiently to BE HAPPY and HAVE POWER. PROPER PEOPLE ARE SAFE from NEEDS which ARE NOT SATISFIED and therefore they MAKE OTHER PEOPLE SAFE because they DO not NEED to ACT UNPREDICTABLY or INCOHERENTLY. They KNOW HOW to DECIDE and how to CHOOSE and therefore they HAVE the RIGHT to DECIDE and CHOOSE for OTHERS who CANNOT CHOOSE, because they DO NOT KNOW or CANNOT DO because they ARE NOT ABLE to.

PROPER PEOPLE ARE IMPARTIAL. Their NEEDS ARE SATISFIED so they NEED NOT CHOOSE "in their OWN BEST INTEREST." Their "BEST IN-TEREST" is BEST MET by WHAT IS and what WILL BE without CHANGE. They CAN DECIDE "on the merits" of the situation without NEEDING to "get something for themSELVES." They HAVE POWER OVER OTHER PEOPLE because they HAVE what they NEED and therefore do not NEED to USE that POWER to SATISFY their OWN NEEDS.

All People ARE EQUAL to ALL OTHER PEOPLE insofar as they ARE PROP-ER PEOPLE. ANY INDIVIDUAL who IS ABLE to KNOW and ABLE to DO CAN BE a PROPER PERSON. He MUST only DO what he SHOULD DO in order to KNOW what he MUST KNOW in order to DO what he MUST DO in order to HAVE what he MUST HAVE in order to BE what he SHOULD BE, what EVERY ADULT CAN BE.

We hold these Truths to be self-evident, that all Men are created Equal, that they are endowed by their Creator with certain inalienable Rights . . . among these are Life, Liberty and the Pursuit of Happiness . . . (*The Declaration of Independence of the United States of America:* July 4, 1776)

CONCLUSION

". . . all Men are created Equal . . ."

The Story of America is, very largely, a prolonged, complex, and sometimes tragic exegesis of those few lines from *The Declaration of Independence.*

"All men are created Equal." Yes, all MEN are EQUAL. But who *exactly* are MEN? And the others, those PEOPLE who ARE NOT MEN, what RIGHTS, what LIBERTY, what FUTURE have those who ARE NOT quite ADULTS?

Over the past two hundred years, more PEOPLE, more KINDS of PEOPLE have insisted that they ARE EQUAL and "entitled to certain inalienable RIGHTS." Black PEOPLE, women, American Indians, Poor PEOPLE and now the OLD and the MORIBUND DEMAND the RIGHT to DECIDE and to DO because they ARE ABLE to KNOW, ABLE to DECIDE. CRIMINALS and the INSANE are INSIST-ING on the RIGHT to be considered CHANGED and HEALTHY and therefore entitled to DECIDE and to DO.

There are still those who CANNOT INSIST, CANNOT DEMAND, are not ABLE TO KNOW or to DO. They remain CHILDREN—without RIGHTS, with-out CHOICE, without FREEDOM, inhibited from pursuing HAPPINESS as they might wish to. Since they DO NOT KNOW, they CANNOT DO and they NEED to be CARED FOR . . . without the ABILITY TO DECIDE, they CANNOT DECIDE and therefore SHOULD NOT DECIDE. Their FUTURE is in the hands of those who DO KNOW, who CAN DECIDE, who TAKE CARE of them. The question remains as painful, as perplexing as ever: EXACTLY which INDIVIDUAL PEOPLE are ENTITLED to LIVE LIFE FREELY PURSUING HAPPINESS as EQUALS of other MEN?

The history of AMERICA is the Story of EXACTLY who HAS the RIGHT to DECIDE EXACTLY who HAS the RIGHT to DECIDE.

141

AFTERWORD: AN AMERICAN'S STORY

Let me tell you a story about why I chose to write about storytelling and especially why I chose to write about different kinds of people telling different kinds of stories.

This is not an attempt to be flippant. Stories are very important and the values in stories are even more important, so telling a story about the value of stories is the best way of talking about them that I know.

When I was little, seven or eight and later, and people would ask me what I was (a common question back then; I don't know if it is still routine to ask kids what they are and expect "Chinese" or "Scottish" or "half-British/half-French" for an answer), anyway, when they'd ask I would say, "half-Italian Catholic, half-Hungarian Jew and one hundred percent American."

Neither side of my family considered themselves "American" when I was growing up. Americans were another kind of people categorized by my mother as cold, pleasure-loving, and unwilling to give you enough to eat when you went to their houses. For my father, Americans were hopelessly naive about the nature of the world; that a drinking country had voted in Prohibition always struck him as the last word in inconsistency and self-deception. Americans were also totally devoid of taste and likely to tell you an off-color joke, ask you if you'd ever been to a baseball game, and invite you for Thanksgiving dinner. He waxed enthusiastic about Yankee ingenuity, however, and loved to be surprised by Americans acting like people. My mother always seemed rather disappointed that they acted like people. She was basically afraid of and intimidated by them, I think, and preferred them to be cold and unwilling to be truly generous. For my father the epitome of Americans being American was "the fake grandmother,": a grandmother who charges her children to babysit for her grandchildren. For my mother what distinguished Americans from people is that they take vacations and spend money on themselves.

And I claimed to be 100 percent American, whatever that means. I guess I took the melting pot seriously and personally. There I was, born in the U.S. of the two most unlikely parents anyone could have. And America really seemed to be the land of possibilities of an otherwise impossible kind. Upward mobility? I'd seen it. My mother worked in the garment district and worked her way up to owning her own shop. She left it all to marry my father, an Intellectual. It didn't work, but that's another story. The land of opportunity? Certainly more than Europe at that time (early 1950's). Freedom? Those were the days of McCarthy, who was a real figure to me and dark muttery stories were heard that seemed very frightening and foreboding. But compared to the stories of gas chambers and concentration camps it just didn't seem that bad. Before I was born, an American passport had been about the best guarantee of safety there was, and I felt inordinately glad from earliest childhood that I was an American and I could get an American passport and cross borders without being afraid.

I knew a lot of Americans, too, of course. I went to a totally American school, meaning that there were no Catholics or Jews in it. It was a private girls school of genteel and Anglican persuasion. We sang "Holy, Holy, Holy," at the drop of a hat, and were expected to jump up from our seats when an adult entered the room and say "good morning Mrs. so and so" in happy unison. There was always some confusion when the janitor came in about whether you were supposed to stand up or not. I knew you weren't supposed to because I knew about those things. It seemed like the richer the girls were, the dumber. When I would visit my mother's relatives in New York, the teachers would say that I'd been with the Wop relatives again, but when my father would come to school they always seemed a bit bewildered. He intimidated them and they thought they owned the world.

When I was growing up we had no money to speak of. My parents were separated and there never seemed to be much to go around. So, my mother took up babysitting. She babysat for the same type of people I went to school with, but she drew the line at sitting for anyone who actually was at the school. Next door, maybe. I went with her. We would go by taxi to some big empty house somewhere and look after the children. As far as I can remember, the children were all blond with skinny legs and limited intelligence. By the time my mother started sitting I was about ten or eleven, and so most of the children were younger than I was, but stupid . . . they were so incredibly limited that I couldn't believe it. I resented the babysitting because I would run out of books to read and these rich people, as my mother called them, didn't have any books. They always lived out in some wretched suburb, too, where there weren't any libraries. But they did have freezers which could keep ice cream and a TV which could get NBC, both lacking and lamented by my mother and myself in our own home. So we would watch TV and eat ice cream after the kids had been put to bed and wait up until some drunk Americans would come home at two or three o'clock in the morning smelling of alcohol and the outside world. Then I'd get my books together and find my homework papers while the man couldn't find his checkbook, and the woman rushed off to bed because she was very tired. And then we'd leave, sometimes in a Mercedes, and sometimes in a filthy taxicab driven usually by Ernie who was a bookie and played the horses and made remarks and was a real person. He may have been Italian or Polish.

So there was all that, and it did not upset me particularly, but it did fascinate me. I never really wondered who was right about anything; they were all so sure that they were right. There was no other way to be or think or see the world my father's every word would say, and likewise my mother's and the school's and the drunken stock-broker's. There was only one world, I could see that, but a thousand views of it. Each view coherent, self-consistent, limiting in some respects, a blessed relief in others. Each existing like a self-satisfied planet revolving around a central star blissfully unaware of who was the center and who the wanderer.

It was a funny way to grow up. Never really socialized, never really a part, never minding not being a part except of course of the best clique at school, taking as truth somehow the best people felt about themselves and the worst anyone else said. I learned to listen very very hard to what people said and what different people said about the same things and I learned that the same facts, the same incidents, the same world was very very different when talked about by different people. The stories, the myths, the anecdotes were different. There was no truth, ever, in my world. Only stories, talk about the truth.

And yet people talked to each other and groups of similar people told similar stories and seemed to accept the versions of people like themselves without any difficulty. My mother and my teacher might see the same incident and talk about it very very differently. However, my mother and her sisters and the woman upstairs would report the same incident the same way, expressing surprise and outrage and relief at all the right points. And the teacher could talk to the other teachers and the WASP American parents and tell them a story which they understood. And I began to learn about which stories to tell to which people and that when you tell a story it is not the events which matter; it's the point which matters. The point says "hey, you and I know the world is like this and so this behavior, this event means this."

And so this book grows out of this story in many ways because it is a book about stories and about finding out what people are really talking about in their stories. It is based on the idea that stories are rooted in what you know to be true and that telling a story to someone who does not share your presuppositions about the world as expressed in that story means that you do not really know what you are talking about or care. When you talk to people who can't understand you, your story gets lost and what happens is that the people you are talking to know you are not one of them. They might put you in some sort of category and say that they never understand the stories Jews tell, or whatnot; more likely, though, they just feel bored and confused.

But I am left with the idea of whether there is an American story, since I just told you a story about different groups in the United States all talking at cross purposes and thinking the others were beyond the pale, if not downright immoral. I think that there is a core of common concerns among Americans, and who should be considered an American involves all those people who consider themselves to be American. Neither of my parents considered themselves American because they knew that they did not share the values of a lot of people whom they categorized as Americans, but those people who consider themselves Americans do share a set of values. Americans would find my father's insistence on taste and on understanding the complexities of the political and economic world overly intellectual and elitist, and my mother's constant self-sacrifice at the cost of her own happiness to be far from reasonable, pathetic, maybe, even if in some sense commendable. And I share those values of those people who call themselves Americans. I believe deep down in *choices,* of the *ability* of the *individual* to *control* his own life in many ways, in the *responsibility* of the *individual* to make his own decisions. Furthermore, I can be moved by arguments that something is *not fair.* I think everyone should have *equal opportunities* and that different people have a *right* to *live their lives their own way as long as they don't hurt anybody else* because somehow people are all equal and have the *right* to *choose* what they want out of life and shouldn't be stopped from getting it from *accidents of birth* which they can't *control.* As long as an *individual* is *competent* he has the *right* to do what he thinks best and *rise as high as he can rise.* And all the rest.

I believe that *individuals* have *rights* and they have the *power* and the *responsibility* to make *decisions* for themselves. Furthermore, I believe that *time* is *sequential,* that events have *causes* which are to be found in either the *facts* of the natural world or in past events. I believe that it is possible to *understand* something and to *explain* it and I have almost a religious belief in the *power* of language to *facilitate change.* If you can *talk about* something you *feel,* then you will *feel better.* If you can *understand* a *problem,* you can solve it.

If you are an American, these beliefs may seem so stupidly trite that you would wonder why anyone would put these things down. You may think that you don't really think they are true. Perhaps some aren't for you. But I would bet that when you argue against one of them, it will be in terms of another. I've never met an American yet who doesn't believe that the individual is the central figure on the stage of the world and even arguments for being unselfish put forward by ten year olds involve being altruistic because even though it helps society, being unselfish makes you feel good and therefore is good for you.

For example, several people I know wrote down their versions of the story "The Boy Who Cried Wolf." In discussing the stories, it turned out that there were differences of opinion about what the story was really about, what the boy had done which meant he had to be punished. One opinion held by a couple of people was that the boy had been irresponsible to his sheep in crying wolf, and, in general, was a bad worker and irresponsible in carrying out his job. I felt that he made the villagers feel like such fools that they were embarrassed to look at each other and so he had disturbed the life of the village in that he disrupted social relations. Though our versions appeared totally odd to each other, there was nothing in the "responsibility" version which I could not understand, though I was surprised at what others thought the story was about (and indeed, in the stories, different aspects of the events and situation were emphasized by different people). They thought it was odd that I should be so concerned with the feelings of the villagers, but that people have feelings and that feelings are important considerations which one can tell a story about was certainly clear to them. That is the level of commonality I think there is among Americans and which defines American culture.

I'm not alone in this belief that American culture exists. It is a *commonsense* widely accepted belief. We can read about it, hear about it on television, talk about it to one another, discuss whether so-and-so is typically American and feel ourselves to be incredibly typical Americans when we go abroad as we find out that the world is inhabited by people who are really much more different from ourselves than we are from each other. Even when we feel more at home in some other country or with some other group we are expressing a rather American idea. Lots of people in all parts of the world are not interested in getting to know how the rest of the world is and would be appalled at the notion that one could possibly feel "at home" somewhere other than where home "is." In other words, Americans really locate their terms of reference inside themselves as individuals more than many other peoples do. It is not the place, the others which determine our happiness, but our own experiences of those situations, what we make of them. This Apologia, Afterword, piece of self-indulgent rhetoric, or whatever, is also American.

Think for a minute about the American psychotherapies which have grown up in the last ten years or so. What do they emphasize? *Communication,* the *here and now,* the *freeing* of the *individual* from the *past* and from ties with family and loved ones which are not *appropriate* anymore. That *relationships* are transitory and should be *held onto* and *worked* for just as long as they have *meaning* in the *individual's* life, and that life moves in *time* and the *individual changes* as *time* moves by. Even more central to why this writing should be seen as American is that it is a confession of why I am involved with my subject, what it means to me.

I believe that we are all, inescapably, part of our work. There is no objectivity, no outside, no place to run to hide one's personal, social, and cultural involvement in what one is doing. What reasons one gives will differ enormously depending on what one can count as a reason in one's world. The form in which one gives that answer will also depend on what can count as a way of presenting a reason. I believe in the *individual,* doing work *honestly* according to his own definition of honesty. And so I present a personal, intuitive, subjective account of the wellsprings of my work in the historical and psychological terms which make sense to me to clothe it in. And why? Because I would like to be able to be objective and I am apologizing because my work is not objective. But I hope by being *open* and *honest* about that lack of objectivity, that the work can be judged, not as a work of a traditional science, but as a work of a new American self-referential, nonobjective science. A science which accepts that the observer is constrained by his system of observing as much as the observed are constrained and that one cannot understand an observation without understanding in some way what that observation means to the observer.

If we do not know that, we don't have enough information about the observations to make them truly interpretable.

A friend of mine told me that she was quite worried about the way in which I chose to look at texts because it was not "linguistic" or "scientific." "How can your comments be disproved?" she asked. I think that the need for proof and disproof results from a faulty idea of objectivity. I do not think there is such a thing as disproving the kinds of comments I have been making in this essay, nor do I think that one ought to *want* to disprove it. I am not presenting you with the TRUTH, I don't believe in the truth, that is what this whole work is about. I do believe, however, that people say things which they believe to be true and which strike a resonant chord in others who share their beliefs about the way things can be true and the way truth can be expressed. Much as we might wish scientific texts to be objective, true for all time, beyond the confines of time or culture, those texts are as culturally constrained as any other. The message of studies in the rhetoric of culture is that there is no outside, no objectivity. As scientists, as text builders, we are constrained to move from where we are to nowhere other than where we are (still).

BIBLIOGRAPHY

Barth, Fredrik. 1975. *Ritual and Knowledge Among the Baktaman of New Guinea.* New Haven: Yale University Press.

Benedict, Ruth. 1967. *The Chrysanthemum and the Sword.* New York: World Publishing Corp.

Brown, Penelope & Stephen Levinson. 1978. "Universals in language Usage: Politeness Phenomena," in *Questions and Politeness Strategies in Social Interaction,* Esther N. Goody (ed.) 56–289. Cambridge: Cambridge University Press.

Colson, Elizabeth. 1971. "Heroism, Martyrdom, and Courage: An Essay on Tonga Ethics," in *The Translation of Culture: Essays to E. E. Evans-Pritchard,* T. O. Beidelman (ed.) 19–35. London: Tavistock Publications.

Eisner, Janet. 1975. *A Grammar of Oral Narrative.* Unpublished University of Michigan Dissertation.

Emery, Stewart with Neal Rogin. 1978. *Actualizations: You Don't Have to Rehearse to Be Yourself.* Garden City, NY: Doubleday & Co., Dolphin Books.

Gillies, Jerry. 1976. *Friends: The Power and Potential of the Company You Keep.* New York: Harper & Row, Barnes and Noble Books.

Goffman, Erving. 1961. *Asylums: Essays on the Social Situation of Mental Patients and Other Inmates.* Garden City, NY: Anchor Books.

————. 1967. *Interaction Ritual: Essays on Face to Face Behavior.* Garden City, New York: Doubleday & Co., Inc.

Greenwald, Dr. Jerry A. 1975. *Creative Intimacy: How to Break the Patterns That Poison Your Relationships.* New York: Simon and Schuster.

Grimes, Joseph. 1982. "Topics within Topics," *Analyzing Discourse: Text and Talk.* D. Tannen (ed.) 164–176. Washington, DC.: Georgetown University Press.

Hopper, Paul & Sandra Thompson. 1980. "Transitivity in Grammar and Discourse," *Language* 56(2), 251–99.

Jefferson, Gail. 1979. "Sequential Aspects of Storytelling in Conversation," in *Studies in the Organization of Conversational Interaction,* J. Schenkein, (ed.) 219–248. New York: Academic Press.

Jones, Larry & Linda K. Jones. 1979. "Multiple Levels of Information in Discourse," in *Discourse Studies in Meso-American Linguistics: Volume 1,* Linda K. Jones (ed.) 3–28. Arlington, TX: Summer Institute of Linguistics.

Joos, Martin. 1968. *The English Verb: Form and Meaning.* Madison, WI: University of Wisconsin Press.

Labov, William. 1972. *Language in the Inner City: Studies in the Black English Vernacular* = *Conduct and Communication* No. 3, 354–396. Philadelphia: University of Pennsylvania Press.

————, and Joshua Waletzky. 1967. "Narrative Analysis: Oral Versions of Personal Experience," in *Essays on the Verbal and Visual Arts,* June Helms, (ed.) 12–44. Seattle: University of Washington Press.

Longacre, Robert E. 1976. *An Anatomy of Speech Notions.* Lisse: The Peter de Ridder Press.

Lotman, Juri M. 1975. "On the Metalanguage of a Typological Description of Culture," *Semiotica 14,* 97–123.

Newman, Mildred & Bernard Berkowitz. 1978. *How to Take Charge of Your Life.* New York: Bantam Books.

Polanyi-Bowditch, Livia. 1976a. "Why the Whats are When: Mutually Contextualized Realms of Narrative," in *Proceedings of the Second Annual Meeting of the Berkeley Linguistics Society,* February 14–16, 1976. K. Whistler, et. al (eds.) 59–78. Berkeley, CA: Berkeley Linguistics Society.

Polanyi, Livia. 1978a. The American Story: Cultural Constraints on the Meaning and Structure of Stories in Conversation. Unpublished Dissertation. University of Michigan.

————. 1978b. "False Starts Can be True" in *Proceedings of the Fourth Annual Meeting of the Berkeley Linguistics Society,* 1978 Jeri Jaeger et. al (eds.) 628–639. Berkeley CA: Berkeley Linguistics Society.

————. 1979. "So What's the Point?" *Semiotica,* 25(3–4), 208–24.

————. 1981. "What Stories Can Tell Us About their Teller's World." *Poetics Today* 2(2), 97–112.

————. & Paul Hopper. forthcoming. "Reconsidering the Foreground Background Distinction," in *Text World, Text Perspective* Jozsef Andor (ed.). Hamburg: Buske.

Putney, Snell & Gail J. Putney. 1972. *The Adjusted American: Normal Neuroses in the Individual and Society.* New York: Harper & Row, Perennial Library.

Rubin, Theodore Isaac. 1967. *The Winner's Notebook.* New York: Collier Books.

Sacks, Harvey. 1972. "On the Analyzability of Stories by Children," in *Directions in Sociolinguistics: The Ethnography of Communication,* John J. Gumperz and Dell Hymes (ed.) 325–45. New York: Holt, Rinehart and Winston.

————. 1974. "An Analysis in the Course of a Joke's Telling in Conversation," in *Explorations in the Ethnography of Speaking,* Richard Bauman and Joel Sherzer (eds.) 337–53. London: Cambridge University Press.

————. "Lecture Notes: Stories in Conversation." University of California. Spring, 1970 and Fall, 1971. Mimeo.

———— & Emanuel Schegloff. 1974. "Opening up Closings," in Roy Turner (ed). 233–254. *Ethnomethodology.* Penguin Books.

————, Emanuel A. Schegloff, & Gail Jefferson. 1974. "A Simplest Systematics for the Organization of Turn-Taking for Conversation." *Language 50,* 696–735.

Schank, Roger & Robert Abelson. 1977. *Scripts, Plans, Goals and Understanding.* Hillsdale, NJ: Lawrence Erlbaum Associates.

Schegloff, Emanuel A. 1971. Notes on Conversational Practice Formulating Place," in *Language and Social Context,* Giglioli (ed.). Penguin Books.

Tannen, Deborah. 1984. *Conversational Style: Analyzing Talk among Friends.* Norwood, NJ: Ablex Publishing Corp.

van Dijk, T. A. (Ed.). In press. *The Handbook of Discourse Analysis.* New York: Academic Press.

Wilensky, Robert. 1978. *Understanding Goal Based Stories.* (Tech Report 140). New Haven: Yale University Computer Science.

Author Index

Italics indicate bibliographic citations.

SUBJECT INDEX